W9-BFG-686

Fodor's InFocus

TURKS & CAICOS ISLANDS

1st Edition

**Where to Stay and Eat
for All Budgets**

**Must-See Sights
and Local Secrets**

Ratings You Can Trust

Fodor's Travel Publications New York, Toronto, London, Sydney, Auckland
www.fodors.com

FODOR'S IN FOCUS TURKS & CAICOS ISLANDS

Series Editor: Douglas Stallings

Editor: Douglas Stallings

Editorial Production: Astrid deRidder

Writer: Ramona Settle

Maps & Illustrations: David Lindroth *cartographer*; Bob Blake and Rebecca Baer, *map editors*

Design: Fabrizio La Rocca, *creative director*; Guido Caroti, *art director*; Ann McBride, *designer*; Melanie Marin, *senior picture editor*

Cover Photo: Philip Coblentz/Brand X Pictures/age fotostock

Production/Manufacturing: Amanda Bullock

COPYRIGHT

SPECIAL SALES

This book is available for special discounts for bulk purchases for sales promotions or premiums. Special editions, including personalized covers, excerpts of existing books, and corporate imprints, can be created in large quantities for special needs. For more information, write to Special Markets/Premium Sales, 1745 Broadway, MD 6-2, New York, New York, NY 10019, or e-mail specialmarkets@randomhouse.com.

AN IMPORTANT TIP & AN INVITATION

Although all prices, opening times, and other details in this book are based on information supplied to us at press time, changes occur all the time in the travel world, and Fodor's cannot accept responsibility for facts that become outdated or for inadvertent errors or omissions. **So always confirm information when it matters,** especially if you're making a detour to visit a specific place. Your experiences—positive and negative—matter to us. If we have missed or misstated something, **please write to us.** We follow up on all suggestions. Contact the Turks & Caicos editor at editors@fodors.com or c/o Fodor's at 1745 Broadway, New York, NY 10019.

PRINTED IN THE UNITED STATES OF AMERICA

10 9 8 7 6 5 4 3 2 1

Be a Fodor's Correspondent

Your opinion matters. It matters to us. It matters to your fellow Fodor's travelers, too. And we'd like to hear it. In fact, we *need* to hear it. When you share your experiences and opinions, you become an active member of the Fodor's community. Here's how you can help improve Fodor's for all of us.

Tell us when we're right. We rely on local writers to give you an insider's perspective. But our writers and staff editors also depend on you. Your positive feedback is a vote to renew our recommendations for the next edition.

Tell us when we're wrong. We update most of our guides every year. But things change. If any of our descriptions are inaccurate or inadequate, we'll incorporate your changes in the next edition and will correct factual errors at fodors.com *immediately*.

Tell us what to include. You probably have had fantastic travel experiences that aren't yet in Fodor's. Why not share them with a community of like-minded travelers? Share your discoveries and experiences with everyone directly at fodors.com. Your input may lead us to add a new listing or a higher recommendation.

Give us your opinion instantly at our feedback center at www.fodors.com/feedback. You may also e-mail editors@fodors.com with the subject line "Turks & Caicos Editor." Or send your nominations, comments, and complaints by mail to Turks & Caicos Editor, Fodor's, 1745 Broadway, New York, NY 10019.

Happy Traveling!

Tim Jarrell, Publisher

CONTENTS

ABOUT
THIS BOOK

Our Ratings

We wouldn't recommend a place that wasn't worth your time, but sometimes a place is so experiential that superlatives don't do it justice: you just have to be there to know. These sights, properties, and experiences get our highest rating, **Fodor's Choice**, indicated by orange stars throughout this book. Black stars highlight sights and properties we deem **Highly Recommended**, places that our writers, editors, and readers praise again and again for consistency and excellence.

Credit Cards

Want to pay with plastic? **AE, D, DC, MC, V** after restaurant and hotel listings indicate whether American Express, Discover, Diners Club, MasterCard, and Visa are accepted.

Restaurants

Unless we state otherwise, restaurants are open for lunch and dinner daily. We mention dress only when there's a specific requirement and reservations only when they're essential or not accepted—it's always best to book ahead.

Hotels

Unless we tell you otherwise, you can assume that the hotels have private bath, phone, TV, and air-conditioning. We always list facilities but not whether you'll be charged an extra fee to use them, so when pricing accommodations, find out what's included.

Many Listings

★ Fodor's Choice
★ Highly recommended
⊠ Physical address
✛ Directions
🕮 Mailing address
☎ Telephone
🖷 Fax
⊕ On the Web
✎ E-mail
🎫 Admission fee
☉ Open/closed times
Ⓜ Metro stations
🚍 Credit cards

Hotels & Restaurants

🏨 Hotel
🛏 Number of rooms
♨ Facilities
🍴 Meal plans
✕ Restaurant
🍴 Reservations
⤢ Smoking
🍺 BYOB
✕🏨 Hotel with restaurant that warrants a visit

Outdoors

🏌 Golf
⛺ Camping

Other

☾ Family-friendly
⇨ See also
🖂 Branch address
☞ Take note

WHEN TO GO

Any time of the year is a great time to go to the Turks and Caicos islands, where the climate is fairly constant year-round.

Peak season is between December 15 and April 15—the same as in the Caribbean—when prices average 20% to 50% higher than in the summer months. This is also when the beaches are most crowded. During the early part of the season, nighttime temperatures may be somewhat cool, requiring a light summer sweater. January through March can bring on the so-called "Christmas winds" and the resulting swells, with higher chances of windy days. If the winds are blowing from the north, Grace Bay Beach will have waves, but you can always go to a beach on the other side of the island if you want calm waters. Water temperatures in the Turks and Caicos are cooler than those in the Caribbean, especially in the months before March.

Climate

Temperatures in the Turks and Caicos islands range from 75°F to 85°F year-round, except perhaps in the hottest months of August and September. The islands are among the driest in the Caribbean and southern Atlantic region, with an average of 350 days of sunshine, light trade winds, and less humidity than in surrounding islands.

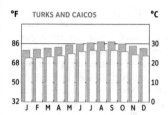

Water temperatures range from the high 70s in the winter to the low 80s in the summer; generally, the water here is cooler than in the Caribbean until March. Of all the islands, North Caicos receives the most rainfall, with about 40 inches per year; the other islands in the archipelago get about 21 inches a year. Unless a tropical front moves through, rain usually consists of brief showers mixed with sunshine; overcast days are highly unusual. As in the Caribbean, the hurricane season runs from June through November. Hurricanes are rare; two hurricanes in September 2008 were the first storms to strike the islands directly in 50 years.

Welcome to the Turks and Caicos

WORD OF MOUTH

"Grace Bay beach in Turks & Caicos was by far the most beautiful beach that I have seen. We stayed close to the middle of the beach and took a long walk down each side of the beach from our hotel. It was gorgeous. The different colors of blue in the water was an amazing sight."

—travelenthusiast

By
Ramona
Settle

THE TURQUOISE-COLORED WATER IN THE TURKS AND CAICOS IS ALMOST ELECTRIC. These islands have some of the most beautiful water in the world, so you can expect almost all of your activities here to be water-based. The beaches are among the most incredible you will ever see. It's not uncommon for visitors to find they have no need for museums, no desire to see ruins, no penchant even to read books. Don't be surprised if you wake up on your last morning and realize you never strayed far from the beach or those mesmerizing views.

A much-disputed legend tells us that Columbus first discovered these islands on his first voyage to the New World in 1492. Although known and explored for longer than most other island groups in the southern Atlantic and Caribbean, the Turks and Caicos islands (pronounced *kay*-kos) still remain part of the less-discovered Caribbean. More than 40 islands—only eight of which are inhabited—make up this self-governing British overseas territory that lies just 575 mi (862 km) southeast of Miami on the third-largest coral reef system in the world.

Although ivory-white, soft, sandy beaches and breathtaking turquoise waters are shared among all the islands, the landscapes are a series of contrasts, from the dry, arid bush and scrub on the flat, coral islands of Grand Turk, Salt Cay, South Caicos, and Providenciales to the greener, foliage-rich undulating landscapes of Middle Caicos, North Caicos, Parrot Cay, and Pine Cay.

The political and historical capital island of the country is Grand Turk, but most of the tourism development is on Providenciales (usually shortened to Provo), thanks to the 12-mi (18-km) stretch of ivory sand that is Grace Bay. Once home to a population of around 500 people plus a few donkey carts, Provo has become a hub of activity since the 1990s, as resorts, spas, and restaurants have been built and as the population has grown to some 15,000. It's the temporary home for the vast majority of visitors who come to the Turks and Caicos islands.

Although most visitors land and stay in Provo, the Turks & Caicos National Museum is in Grand Turk. The museum tells the history of the islands that have, at one time or another, been claimed by the French, Spanish, and British as well as many pirates, long before the predominately North American visitors discovered its shores.

1

Marks of the country's colonial past can be found in the wood-and-stone Bermudian-style clapboard houses—often wrapped in deep-red bougainvillea—that line the streets on the quiet islands of Grand Turk, Salt Cay, and South Caicos. Donkeys roam free in and around the islands' many salt ponds, which are a legacy from a time when residents worked hard as both slaves and then paid laborers to rake salt (then known as "white gold") bound for the United States and Canada.)n Salt Cay the remains of wooden windmills are now home to large osprey nests. On Grand Turk and South Caicos the crystal-edge tidal ponds are regularly visited by flocks of rose-pink flamingos hungry for the shrimp to be found in the shallow, briny waters.

Sea Island cotton, believed to be the highest quality, was produced on the Loyalist plantations in the Caicos Islands from the 1700s. The native cotton plants can still be seen among the stone remains of former plantation houses in the more fertile soils of Middle Caicos and North Caicos. Here the remaining tiny settlements have retained age-old skills using fanner grasses, silver palms, and sisal to create exceptional straw baskets, bags, mats, and hats.

In all, only 25,000 people live in the Turks and Caicos islands; more than half are "Belongers," the term for the native population, mainly descended from African and Bermudian slaves who settled here beginning in the 1600s. The majority of residents work in tourism, fishing, and offshore finance, as the country is a haven for the overtaxed. Indeed, for residents and visitors, life in "TCI" is anything but taxing. While most visitors come to do nothing—a specialty in the islands—this does not mean there's nothing to do.

HISTORY OF THE ISLANDS

For such a small archipelago, the islands of the Turks and Caicos are rich in history. You can go to the excellent museum in Grand Turk, which contains artifacts from the original Lucayan people, pirate treasures, and a replica of the capsule in which John Glenn orbited Earth; or you can explore rock carvings, plantation ruins, or under the sea.

Both San Salvador in the Bahamas and Grand Turk make the claim that Columbus first made landfall in the Americas there in 1492. Although not proven, many scholars believe that Columbus discovered the Americas on Grand Turk. He was greeted by the resident Lucayans, who

Fun Facts

■ JoJo the dolphin, the unofficial mascot of Turks and Caicos, has been around since the early 1990s. He's usually spotted anywhere between Club Med and beyond to the cays. He currently has a girlfriend and baby, and all three of them will swim up to excursion boats.

■ Chalk Sound has the most intensely turquoise color in the world; it is the brightest blue you'll ever see.

■ The Infinity Bar at Anacaona—the longest bar in the world—appears to spill into the ocean.

■ The Turks & Caicos Conch Farm, the only commercial conch farm in the world, is a popular tourist spot. Although it was severely damaged during Hurricane Ike in September 2008, it was being recon-

structed at this writing.

■ The Turks Head Mansion in Grand Turk, now a hotel, has been the location for countless movies. TV stars whose faces you recognize have all filmed here. Most of these movies have been seen on "Lifetime"; now that you know the setting, you'll recognize the background.

■ Rock carvings all over the islands are reputed to be maps to hidden treasures from pirate days. To date, no treasure has been found.

■ Clouds over the Caicos Banks appear to be turquoise in color. That's because the banks are so shallow and bright that they actually reflect on the underside of the clouds. It's the only place in the world to experience this phenomenon.

had lived on these islands for generations. Columbus, along with later shipwrecked Europeans, brought new diseases to the Lucayans, and they were wiped out in a single generation.

Ponce de León may have passed through the Turks and Caicos in 1512, when he made his voyage in search of the Fountain of Youth, and maps from as early as 1530 show the islands, but the Turks and Caicos don't often appear in the historical record during the 1500s and 1600s. However, the 18th century was a colorful era, when pirate ships and Spanish galleons sailed and fought in these waters. It's estimated that some 1,000 shipwrecks surround the islands.

The Turks and Caicos have been claimed by France and Spain, and by Bermuda in the late 1600s. Bermuda wanted the islands for their salt—at the time it was as highly sought after as gold—and for land on which to grow cotton.

The 1700s were a tumultuous time for the Turks and Caicos and the era when piracy first began to be a force. In 1718 two female pirates, Anne Bonny and Mary Read, captured a Spanish treasure ship and its cargo, then settled on Pirate Cay, which is now known as Parrot Cay. In 1720 a pirate by the name of Francoise L'Olonnois lived on French Cay, which he used as a base to raid passing ships. On Providenciales, at Splitting Rock (sometimes called Osprey Rock), there are carvings on the rocks that are reputedly maps to buried treasures. In 1783 the French seized Grand Turk again, but the islands were restored to Britain by the Treaty of Versailles.

In the early 1800s the settlers, who were British loyalists, set up cannons on Fort George Cay in anticipation of attacks by either pirates or the Americans. The cannons are still here, underwater, and can be seen on a boating or snorkeling excursion. In 1834 Britain granted freedom to all slaves in British colonies, and many of the ex-slaves settled in the Turks and Caicos. The economy of the islands also changed during this period. In the mid- to late 1800s, the Turks Island Whaling Company began harpooning and killing whales at Ambergris Cay. Even with an international ban, there were reports of whaling as late as 1960. In 1874 Turks and Caicos were annexed to Jamaica, but when Jamaica gained independence in 1962 Turks and Caicos chose to remain a British Crown colony, and remains so to this day.

In 1962, after orbiting the earth, John Glenn splashed down near Grand Turk. A replica of his capsule is on display outside the airport. Although the islands gained a lot of publicity in the early 1960s, tourism did not really begin until 1967, when the Third Turtle Inn opened as the first hotel on Providenciales; however, it was still a couple of years before the airport was completed. The islands gained additional attention in the early 1980s; shortly after a huge pirate treasure was found in the Silver Shoals north of Hispaniola, a 16th-century wreck—worth millions—was found at Molasses Reef in West Caicos. The island's first large resort, the Club Med, opened in 1984; television arrived in 1985.

Of Wrecks and Treasures

Wrecks have played an important role in the history of the Turks and Caicos. Some island residents can trace their ancestry back to the wreck of the Spanish slave ship *Trouvadore*, which was wrecked off the shore of East Caicos in 1841; because Britain had abolished the slave trade, the surviving slaves were free. But the most famous wreck discovered in these waters is probably of the Spanish galleon *Nuestra Senora de la Concepcion*, which sank after hitting a shallow reef in 1641 in the Silver Shoals—the famous waters between Hispaniola (the island that today is comprised of Haiti and Dominican Republic) and the Turks and Caicos. By 1687 William Phips had recovered a small portion of the treasure, but the larger part still lay undiscovered in the ocean's depths. The bulk of the wreck was not discovered until 1978, by Burt Webber, who had dedicated his life to the quest and had spent some $250,000 to find it. His investment paid off: the wreck contained treasure worth millions, as well as priceless artifacts, including porcelain from the late Ming period. Sadly, Webber was forced to surrender much of the wealth to the government of the Dominican Republic. A third expedition in the late 1990s by Tracey Bowden yielded even more treasure.

GEOGRAPHY, FLORA, AND FAUNA OF THE ISLANDS

Providenciales appears flat, dry, and scrubby, as do most of the Turks and Caicos islands. But first impressions can be deceiving. A closer inspection reveals a wide range of flora and fauna. The landscape is flat—even the hills aren't very high—and dry; although not a true desert, the Turks and Caicos chain experiences the least amount of rainfall of any island in the southern Atlantic and Caribbean. Tropical downpours may last 30 minutes, but then the sun comes out and shines brightly once again. And for many days Provo may see little rain at all; the island has been known to go almost a month with no rain. The sand around the shoreline is made up of crushed coral stone, which is a bright white and makes the sea appear more turquoise than almost anywhere else in the Caribbean.

The official national plant is the Turks head cactus, so named because of its shape. The body is round, and it's topped with a red cylinder, which resembles a Turkish fez

1

(hat). They're found on all the islands, but the best place to see fields of them is on Ambergris Cay. Silver palms grow naturally in the scrub, adding a tropical flair to beaches such as Half Moon Bay, but the trees are most numerous on West Caicos. North Caicos is considered the "garden" island, as it receives the most rainfall of the islands and is greener as a result. The cays all have small limestone cliffs that have formed from years of ocean waves.

French Cay is a bird-watcher's dream, protected as a national park. Here you will see dozens of white-cheeked pintail, reddish egrets, and osprey. The country's national bird, the osprey, can be seen on all the islands, but osprey nests are easier to see at Three Mary Cays on North Caicos or at Splitting Rock, also known as Osprey Rock, on Provo. Bright pink flamingos can be spotted on some islands, especially at Flamingo Pond at North Caicos, the pond at West Caicos, and at Provo's only golf course. Giant blue land crabs come out in the spring after rains. The crabs are huge; a 10-year-old child might need two hands to hold one up. You're more likely to spot one on the sparsely populated islands of North and Middle Caicos, although they can be seen on Provo, too. A crab farm in Greenich Creek on North Caicos grows Caribbean king crabs.

The queen conchs that thrive in the flats between Provo and Little Water Cay are an important part of the islands' economies. The Turks and Caicos have the largest population of conch in the world, and conch is the most important food on these islands. You can take a conch-diving excursion, which might include a conch salad lunch on an isolated beach. Visitors are allowed to bring back home two empty shells per person. No live animals may be brought into the United States, only shells. Conch diving and deep-sea fishing both require fishing permits.

The most important indigenous species of the Turks and Caicos is the rock iguana. They're mostly found at Little Water Cay, which is also known as Iguana Island. So beloved are these iguanas that Little Water Cay has been declared a national park. Excursion companies will make a stop to view them, but you'll pay an additional $5 fee to help protect them.

WHAT'S WHERE

Surrounded by pristine coral reefs with abundant marine life, the Turks and Caicos were initially popular as a pre-eminent dive destination until the development of upscale and luxury resorts on Providenciales in the 1990s. While the divers still come, just a many visitors now come for the resorts and their amenities.

Providenciales. Provo has the lion's share of accommodations in the Turks and Caicos and gets the lion's share of visitors. Come if you are seeking miles of soft sand and luxurious accommodations with the latest technology to keep you comfortable and entertained. Come if you love crystal-clear water and fine dining in gorgeous settings. Don't come for nightlife or shopping—there are few hot spots and even fewer fancy boutiques. Be sure to bring your wallet, though, because everything has to be imported.

The Caicos & the Cays. The private-island resorts are ultra-luxurious, but accommodations on many of the cays are far less ritzy. South Caicos is all about diving; on North and Middle Caicos, you'll feel like you're stepping back in time to a simpler Caribbean. Come here if you like to explore and get away from it all, if you like life to proceed at a really slow pace. If you can afford it, the pampering at Parrot Cay and the Meridien Club might liven things up a bit for you.

Grand Turk. Although the capital of the Turks and Caicos has some well-preserved buildings (not to mention the national museum), the number of visitors has exploded with the building of a major cruise-ship port facility (though the vast majority of these visitors are still single-day cruise passengers). Come here if you like to dive and people-watch at the cruise-ship port. Don't come for luxury accommodations with plenty of amenities. But if you're on a budget, you'll find that prices (particularly for lodging) are more reasonable than those on Provo.

Salt Cay. Step off the ferry or plane here, and you may feel as if you landed in 1950. Come to relax on the prettiest beach in all the Turks and Caicos, and to meet people who might become lifelong friends. In season, you may want to watch whales—it's one of the best places in the world to do so. Don't come expecting more than rustic accommodations and patchy service. But by the time your vacation here is over, your blood pressure will thank you.

IF YOU LIKE...

1

THE BEST BEACHES IN THE WORLD

The main reason most people come to Turks and Caicos is for the beautiful beaches, which make everyone's top ten list. At least one of these beaches will make yours, too. These flat, dry islands with fine coral sand are surrounded by crystal-clear waters that appear almost neon blue. The water is so bright in some places that it glows. And when you think the beach can't be better or prettier than the last one you were on, it is. If you're lucky, sometimes you might have a beautiful strand all to yourself.

And even amidst the general beauty, some places stand out. People come to Turks and Caicos to see Grace Bay: 12 miles of uninterrupted neon blue, with no rocks or seaweed, and powder-fine sand that won't burn your feet even in the heat of the day. If you can break away from Grace Bay, you'll be rewarded with many other exquisite strands right on Provo. Malcolm's Beach has even bluer water (you must brave the rutted road that leads to it), and Pelican Beach has tons of bright-white conch shells to choose from (though you are limited to only two). On any of the cays you may have the beaches to yourself. Half Moon Bay and Fort George are a photographer's delight, with curving sand, shells, and palms. Pine Cay might have one of the best strands: no rocks, just a long, secluded, gorgeous beach. Mudjin Harbor on Middle Caicos is the most scenic, surrounded by towering cliffs and isolated coves; around one T-shaped coral cliff, waves crash on one side while the other is as calm as glass; at high tide the water meets in the middle. The most beautiful beach of all is North Beach on Salt Cay; with its perfect-color water and clean soft sand, you'll never want to leave.

THE BEST DEEP-SEA FISHING

A Turks and Caicos vacation is all about being on the water. From the bright turquoise waters to the beautiful mangroves to the flats of the Caicos Bank, you can have your pick of watery environments. And one of the best ways to experience the best of Turks and Caicos is to take one of the many fishing excursions. Deep-sea, bone-, or bottom fishing are your choices, and a boat will allow you to see otherwise unreachable parts of the islands.

Bonefishing is exciting. Bonefish live in shallow flats offering unsurpassed views of the smaller cays and Middle Caicos. You'll get an up-close look at mangroves and the wildlife. The fishing itself is challenging and exciting. Your casting technique and endurance will be tested by the bonefish—they're relentless fighters. The key to a great trip is a great guide, and Arthur Dean at Silverdeep is one of the best. His extensive knowledge of the Turks and Caicos flats and his respect for the wildlife and the environment will leave you feeling that your money was well spent.

EXCELLENT DIVING

With the third-largest barrier reef in the world, dramatic walls that drop from 20 feet to more than 6,000 feet, and mostly sunny days shining on crystal-clear, calm waters, the Turks and Caicos are a diver's dream destination. The steep sea walls so close to shore usually prevent waves from churning the water, and sea creatures thrive on these reefs. The visibility is consistently some of the best in the world, averaging 100 to 200 feet on most days. The Turks and Caicos were put on the map as a dive destination, and these waters are still one of the great places in the world to dive.

Each island in the archipelago boasts excellent dive spots. Providenciales has terrific reefs at Northwest Point. West Caicos has Spanish galleon shipwrecks and sudden drop-offs that are so deep they appear to be purple from the surface. Grand Turk has dramatic walls close to shore, so you can spend more time diving and less time reaching the sites. Salt Cay not only has sections of pristine reef that you will have virtually all to yourself, but the immediate area has excellent wreck diving and offers one of the best opportunities in the world to swim with whales in season. The best of the best is probably South Caicos, which claims to have the best visibility in the world, not to mention miles of untouched reefs waiting to be discovered. Expect to see sharks, dolphins, colorful reef fish, stingrays, and lobsters wherever you dive.

GREAT SNORKELING

If you're not a certified diver, then the next-best thing (and perhaps the very best thing for most) is to take a half- or full-day snorkeling excursion to one of the many unin-habited cays and secluded coves. There are many com-

1

panies to choose from, and all the trips can give you a great experience. Some trips are on catamarans, some on powerboats. Some companies allow you to dive for conch, some to snorkel for sand dollars. Some boats stop at Iguana Island to see the iguanas, some stop to let you snorkel on the reef, some stop to find the cannons in the water. But all stop on one of the cays so you can experience a quiet, secluded beach.

If you want a more private experience, then have a boat drop you off on one of many secluded beaches for the day, leaving you with a cooler full of food and drink, along with beach chairs, umbrellas, and snorkel gear. Then you can snorkel directly from the beach. You'll often be alone. Half Moon Bay is one of the most pristine spots for this kind of beach day, with sugar-white sand that lends itself to excellent swimming, brilliant snorkeling, and opportunities to walk and explore on land. Limestone cliffs frame the cove, and iguanas are the only residents. If you budget for only one trip, then go here.

A NEW ISLAND EVERY DAY

With eight inhabited islands, you can visit a different island every day of your weeklong stay in the Turks and Caicos. From Provo's Walkin Marina, you can take the daily ferry over to North Caicos, rent a car, and go on a quest to find secluded beaches. If you rent a car on North Caicos, you can drive over the causeway to Middle Caicos to visit limestone caves or hike the trails next to its glorious coves. During whale-watching season (mid-January to mid-April), you can hop over to Salt Cay, where whales get so close you can reach out and touch them. One of the best day trips is to Grand Turk, with its laid-back charm and Old Caribbean architecture.

Air Turks and Caicos offers early-morning flights to Grand Turk that return the same day. It's only a 20-minute flight to the tiny island, and touring everything Grand Turk has to offer will leave plenty of time for the beach. You can stroll down Front Street to see its original clapboard buildings, and say hi to the wild horses and roosters that share the walk with you. You can stop at the beautiful Anglican church with its bright white walls and even brighter red gate and walk past the bright-pink government house. Don't forget to stop at the excellent museum. There's a lighthouse at the tip of the island. You can swim with

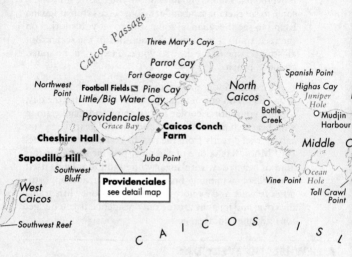

↖ TO BAHAMAS

Caicos Passage

Three Mary's Cays

Parrot Cay
Fort George Cay

Northwest
Point

Football Fields ☒ Pine Cay
Little/Big Water Cay

Providenciales
Grace Bay

Cheshire Hall ◆

Sapodilla Hill ◆
Southwest
Bluff

West
Caicos

Southwest Reef

☒ **Molasses Reef**

**Caicos Conch
Farm** ◆

Juba Point

North
Caicos

○ Bottle
Creek

Spanish Point

Highas Cay
Juniper
Hole

○ Mudjin
Harbour

Middle C

Ocean
Hole

Vine Point

Toll Crawl
Point

| **Providenciales**
see detail map |

C A I C O S   I S L

CAICOS

BANK

SEAL

White Cay

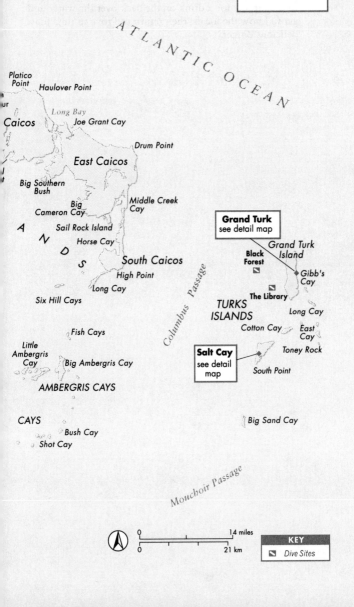

The Turks & Caicos

ATLANTIC OCEAN

Platico Point
Haulover Point
Long Bay
Caicos
Joe Grant Cay
Drum Point
East Caicos
Big Southern Bush
Big Cameron Cay
Middle Creek Cay
Sail Rock Island
A   N   D   S
Horse Cay
South Caicos
High Point
Long Cay
Six Hill Cays
Fish Cays
Little Ambergris Cay
Big Ambergris Cay
AMBERGRIS CAYS
CAYS
Bush Cay
Shot Cay

Grand Turk
see detail map

Grand Turk Island

Black Forest

The Library

Gibb's Cay

TURKS ISLANDS

Long Cay

Cotton Cay
East Cay

Toney Rock

Salt Cay
see detail map

South Point

Columbus Passage

Big Sand Cay

Mouchoir Passage

0   14 miles
0   21 km

KEY
◪ Dive Sites

peaceful stingrays on an excursion to Gibbs Cay. If there's a cruise ship at the port you can shop at the Ron Jon surf shop, Piranha Joe's, and the largest Margaritaville (and store) in the world. Stop at the Sand Bar on the way back to the airport for a drink on the deck over the water and get to know the locals, then return to Provo in time for a delicious dinner.

Providenciales

WORD OF MOUTH

"Definitely Grace Bay in Provo. The whitest sand and clearest water I have ever seen."

—Adkmud

"[T]ake a look at Provo for that perfect soft sand, the coral disintegrates into the softest powder! Also it never gets hot to the touch."

—Virginia

By
Ramona
Settle

PASSENGERS TYPICALLY BECOME SILENT when their plane starts its descent to the Providenciales airport, mesmerized by the shallow, crystal-clear, turquoise waters of Chalk Sound National Park. This island, nicknamed Provo, was once called Blue Hills, after its first settlement. Just south of the airport and downtown area, Blue Hills remains most like a traditional Caicos Island settlement on this, the most developed part of the island chain. Most of the modern resorts, exquisite spas, water-sports operators, shops, business plazas, restaurants, bars, cafés, and the championship golf course are on or close by the 12-mi (18-km) stretch of Grace Bay. In spite of the ever-increasing number of taller and grander condominium resorts—either completed or under construction—it's still possible to find deserted stretches on this priceless, ivory-white shoreline. For guaranteed seclusion, rent a car and explore the southern shores and western tip of the island, or set sail for a private island getaway on one of the many deserted cays nearby.

Providenciales, which has the highest concentration of resorts as well as the country's biggest airport, is where most tourists are headed when they come to the Turks and Caicos. Regardless of which other island you may be going to, you'll stop here first. Accommodations and dining here are expensive; Provo is an upscale destination. Even souvenirs are costly; you won't find T-shirts for under $25, for example. But you won't be hassled here as you might be in less expensive destinations. Beach vendors won't approach you—you have to approach them to buy. Provo is a great place to de-stress and unwind.

Progress and beauty come at a price: there is considerable construction on the island at this writing. But don't worry—you'll still enjoy the gorgeous beaches and wonderful dinners. Although you may start to believe that every road leads to a construction site (or is under construction itself), there are, happily, plenty of sections of beach where you can escape the din.

THE ELUSIVE GREEN FLASH. Does it really exist? You may hear that just as the sun sets on the horizon, on nights where the conditions are perfect, you can see a flash of neon-green light. If you blink, you'll miss it. Your best chance to spot it is on a cloudless day with no haze—and you must have a clear view of the sun as it sinks below the horizon. There is much debate whether this phenomenon exists. Some islanders claim to have seen it; oth-

ers are skeptical. If you want to catch the elusive green flash, Provo—with little haze and often a clear view of the horizon—is one of the best places to try.

EXPLORING PROVIDENCIALES

While you may be quite content to enjoy the beaches and top-notch amenities of Provo's resorts, there are activities beyond the resorts. Provo is a great starting point for island-hopping tours by sea or by air as well as fishing and diving trips. Resurfaced roads make for easy travel.

PLANNING YOUR TIME

PROVIDENCIALES IN 1 DAY

Rent a high-clearance vehicle and go around the island for a day. Start at Pelican Beach in search of empty conch shells. Then check out the Conch Farm, the only one in the world. From the Conch Farm, stop to see "The Hole" in Long Bay on your way to the other end of the island. You can also stop and see Cheshire Hill on your way to Chalk Sound. Chalk Sound is the island's one must-see. The water here is shallow and bright with small, mushroom-like islands in the middle, like a miniature Palau; the sight takes your breath away. Check out Sapodilla Bay and Taylor Bay, where the waters are shallow for hundreds of yards, making them a child's dream. Afterward, take the long, bumpy road to Sapodilla Hill, also known as Osprey Rock; there you can search for rock carvings that are reputedly maps for pirate treasures. While you are there, take a ride to Malcolm's Beach, where just getting there is the adventure. Finish the afternoon at Blue Hills, where colorful buildings are the setting for a game of "slamming" dominos.

WHAT TO SEE

☼ **Caicos Conch Farm.** On the northeast tip of Provo, this is a major mariculture operation, where mollusks are farmed commercially (more than 3 million conch are here). It's a popular tourist attraction too, offering guided tours and a small gift shop selling conch-related souvenirs, jewelry, and freshwater pearls. At this writing, the conch farm had just reopened after severe damage from Hurricane Ike in September 2008. Repairs will be ongoing through at least part of 2009. ⊠*Leeward-Going-Through, Leeward* ☎*649/946–5330* ⊕*www.caicosconchfarm.com* ⊠*$6* ☼*Mon.–Sat. 9–4.*

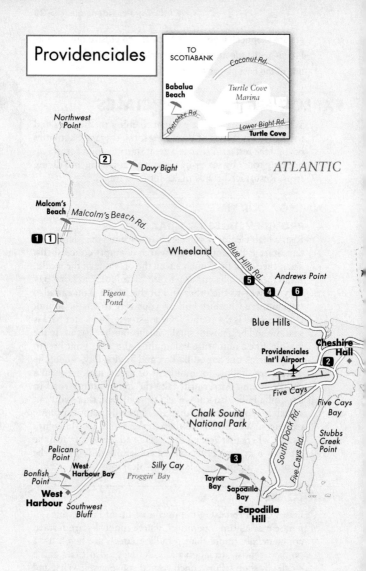

Providenciales

TO SCOTIABANK

Coconut Rd.

Babalua Beach

Turtle Cove Marina

Cherokee Rd.

Lower Bight Rd.

Turtle Cove

Northwest Point

ATLANTIC

2 *Davy Bight*

Malcom's Beach

Malcom's Beach Rd.

1 1

Wheeland

Blue Hills Rd.

5

Andrews Point

4 6

Pigeon Pond

Blue Hills

Cheshire Hall

Providenciales Int'l Airport

2

Five Cays

Chalk Sound National Park

Five Cays Bay

Stubbs Creek Point

South Dock Rd.

Five Cays Rd.

Pelican Point

West Harbour Bay

Silly Cay

Proggin' Bay

3

Bonfish Point

West Harbour

Southwest Bluff

Taylor Bay

Sapodilla Bay

Sapodilla Hill

KEY

Beaches
1 Restaurants
1 Hotels

0   2 miles
0   2 km

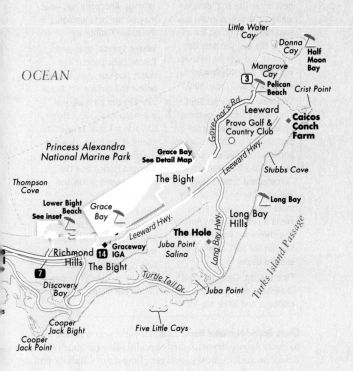

Water Cay

Little Water Cay

Donna Cay

Half Moon Bay

3

Mangrove Cay

Pelican Beach

Crist Point

OCEAN

Leeward

Provo Golf & Country Club

◆ **Caicos Conch Farm**

Princess Alexandra National Marine Park

Grace Bay See Detail Map

Leeward Hwy.

Stubbs Cove

Thompson Cove

The Bight

Long Bay

Lower Bight Beach See inset

Grace Bay

Leeward Hwy.

Long Bay Hills

The Hole

Juba Point Salina

Long Bay Hwy.

Turks Island Passage

//Richmond Hills

◆ **Graceway IGA** **14**

The Bight

7

Discovery Bay

Turtle Tail Dr.

Juba Point

Cooper Jack Bight

Five Little Cays

Cooper Jack Point

Governor's Rd.

Hotel	Aqua Bar & Terrace, **10**	Matsuri Sushi Bar, **14**
Amanyara, **1**	Baci Ristorante, **11**	The Restaurant at Amanyara, **1**
Nikki Beach Resort, **3**	Corner Café, **13**	Sailing Paradise, **4**
Northwest Point Resort, **2**	Da Chonch Shack, **6**	Sharkbites Bar & Grill, **12**
Turtle Cove Inn, **4**	Hole in the Wall, **2**	Smokey's on Da Bay, **15**
	Las Brisas, **3**	Tiki Hut, **8**
Restaurants	Magnolia Wine Bar & Restaurant, **9**	
Angela's Top o' the Cove, **7**		

TOP REASONS TO GO

Grace Bay Beach. The beach is the Turks and Caicos' biggest draw. The soft, powder-white sand with crystal-clear seas seems to go on for as far as the eye can see. Be warned: you will fall in love with this beach and want to come back and retire here.

Snorkel, Scuba, and Snuba. The world's third-largest reef system here makes for an underwater dream. Beginners and experts alike can snorkel right off the beach at Coral Gardens and Smith's Reef. The visibility is ideal, usually more than 100 feet. If you aren't a certified diver, Snuba is a choice for you; the tanks stay on the surface while you explore below.

Fine Dining. On quiet islands like Provo, dining is your nightlife. And while the food is incredible across the island, what really stand out are the settings. Anocoana has what may be the best ambience in the entire Caribbean.

Water Sports. Turks and Caicos are all about the water, and not always what's below the surface. On Grace Bay you can parasail, ride a banana boat, sail a Hobie Cat, ride a kayak, or learn to windsurf. Long Bay Beach is the place to go kite surfing. Leeward Marina and the cays are great skiing and tubing areas.

The Perfect Night Out. At sunset, have a drink at Grace Bay Beach; end the night watching Daniel and Nadine sing at Da Conch Shack, O'Soleil, or Tiki Hut (depending on the night).

Chalk Sound National Park. This is a sight you will not want to miss. As you drive toward Sapodilla Bay on South Dock Road, on your right you will get glimpses of Chalk Sound. The water here is the brightest turquoise you'll ever see, and the mushroom-like tiny islands make the colors even bolder. There are a couple of places to stop for pictures, or you can enjoy lunch overlooking it at Las Brisas Restaurant. No matter how many times you see it, it manages to take your breath away. ⊠*Chalk Sound Rd., Chalk Sound.*

Cheshire Hall. Standing eerily just west of downtown Provo are the remains of a circa-1700 cotton plantation owned by Loyalist Thomas Stubbs. A trail weaves through the ruins, where a few inadequate interpretive signs tell the story of the island's doomed cotton industry with very little information about the plantation itself. A variety of local plants are also identified. To visit, you must arrange for a

On a Budget

CLOSE UP

If you would like to visit one of the world's most beautiful beaches but feel you can't afford this expensive destination, there are ways to save money in the Turks and Caicos and still have an enjoyable trip. Online agents Travelocity, Expedia, and Orbitz can save you a few hundred dollars on a vacation package that combines airfare and hotel (and perhaps a car rental). Traveling during nonpeak seasons, when many resorts offer free nights and extra perks, is another way to save. The discount season coincides with hurricane season, so consider purchasing travel insurance. If you don't mind being a block from the beach, you can even save more.

Once on the island there are other ways to save. Most resort rooms and condos have refrigerators and microwaves, so you can stock up at the supermarket. Graceway IGA has awesome rotisserie chicken and prepared pasta and potato salads. Airlines will allow you to bring a cooler of food as long as perishables are frozen and vacuum sealed; despite airline charges for checked bags, this strategy could save you some money, especially on meat.

At restaurants, dinner might be more expensive than for the same entrée at lunchtime, so arrive 15 minutes before the switch-over and order from the lunch menu. Mango Reef offers four-course prix-fixe meals for a reasonable price. Every Wednesday night at Tiki Hut the $13 ribs are a bargain. You can also pick up food at Pizza Pizza and have a balcony picnic. The best excursion is free: snorkeling off the beach at Coral Gardens.

A good source for events and specials is ⊕ www.TCIEnews.com.

---

tour through the Turks & Caicos National Trust. The lack of context can be disappointing for history buffs; a visit to North Caicos Wades Green Plantation or the Turks & Caicos National Museum could well prove a better fit. ✉ Leeward Hwy., behind Ace Hardware ☎649/941–5710 for National Trust ⊕www.turksandcaicos.tc/nationaltrust �$5 ⊙Daily, by appointment.

The Hole. There are homemade signs leading you to this phenomenon in Long Bay. As you walk around the coral hills, use caution since you will suddenly come upon "The Hole." Through the years the limestone cliffs have sunk, creating a hole that drops 40 feet. Do not bring young children here, as it's not well marked and they could fall through. ✉ Long Bay Rd., Long Bay

  ☾ **Sapodilla Hill.** On this cliff overlooking the secluded Sapodilla Bay you can discover rocks carved with the names of shipwrecked sailors and dignitaries from TCI's maritime and colonial past. There are carvings on the rocks that some claim are secret codes and maps to hidden treasures; many have tried in vain to find these treasures. The hill is known by two other names, Osprey Rock and Splitting Rock. The less adventurous can see molds of the carvings at Provo's International Airport. ✉ *Off South Dock Rd., west of South Dock.*

WHERE TO EAT

Food choices on Provo are numerous, even for picky eaters. With over 50 restaurants to choose from, they run the gamut. Expats from Thailand have opened a Thai restaurant; an expat from Japan owns a Japanese sushi spot. There is an Irish pub, and a restaurant that serves Spanish tapas. You'll find everything from small beach shacks with the freshest seafood right off the boats to elegant restaurants with the best bottles of wine. Most of the restaurants that cater to tourists offer numerous choices, with a little bit of everything on the menu. Don't like seafood? Have chicken or beef. Don't like spice? Ask for the tamer version. Vegetarian? Need kid-friendly food? Feel free to ask for something that's not on the menu; most of the island's chefs will try to accommodate requests. There are excellent caterers on the island too. You can have Gourmet Goods or Kissing Fish Catering pack a picnic lunch or cater a party on the beach. Some restaurants will also set up a table on the beach surrounded by tiki torches for that special romantic dinner. Restaurants on Provo are generally upscale and expensive; you will find no chains or fast-food places here.

You can spot the island's Caribbean influence everywhere. Local food is heavy on seafood, usually the catch of the day right off local boats, including lobster during the season that runs from August through March. It is illegal for restaurants to serve lobster out of season, so you will not find it on local menus from April to July. The best local food on the island is conch, which you will find everywhere prepared in many different ways. You may find it raw in a salad, as fried conch fingers, in spicy conch fritters, or in hearty conch chowder. It is often a part of fresh seafood specials, with colorful presentation and a tangy dose of spice.

Pick up a free copy of *Where When How's Dining Guide*, which you will find all over the island; it contains menus, Web sites, and pictures of all the restaurants.

WHAT IT COSTS				
¢	$	$$	$$$	$$$$
RESTAURANTS				
under $8	$8–$12	$12–$20	$20–$30	over $30

Restaurant prices are for a main course at dinner and include any taxes or service charges.

GRACE BAY

$$$$ ✕**Anacaona.** At the Grace Bay Club, this palapa-shaded restaurant has become a favorite of the country's chief minister. But despite the regular presence of government bigwigs, the restaurant continues to offer a memorable dining experience minus the tie, the air-conditioning, and the attitude. Start with a bottle of fine wine; then enjoy the light and healthy Mediterranean-influenced cuisine. The kitchen utilizes the island's bountiful seafood and fresh produce. Oil lamps on the tables, gently revolving ceiling fans, and the murmur of the trade winds add to the Edenic environment. The entrancing ocean view and the careful service make it an ideal choice when you want to be pampered. It's a good thing the setting is amazing; portions are tiny, so you're paying for ambience. Just added: the world's first Infinity Bar, which seems to spill right into the ocean. Children under 12 are not allowed. Long pants and collared shirts are required. ✉*Grace Bay Club, Grace Bay* ☎*649/946–5050* ⚍*Reservations essential* ⚌*AE, D, MC, V.*

$$$ ✕**Atlantic Bar & Grill.** What sets this casual restaurant apart from the rest is that all the entrées are cooked on outdoor grills within view. If you aren't hungry when you arrive, just wait until you smell the grilled meats; the aromas alone will make you salivate. Fish, lamb, and steaks are best simply grilled, but ask for extra sauce; there usually isn't enough to cover the entrées. Lunch here is a standout, especially the lunch-sized rib-eye steak with grilled vegetables. ✉ *West Bay Club Resort, Lower Bight Rd., Lower Bight* ☎*649/946–8550* ⚌*AE, D, DC, M, V.*

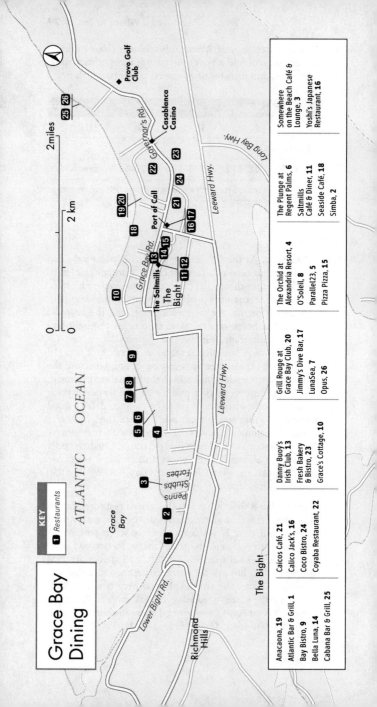

Grace Bay Dining

KEY
1 *Restaurants*

2miles

2 km

ATLANTIC OCEAN

Grace Bay

Penns
Stubbs
Forbes

Richmond
Hills

Lower Bight Rd.

The Bight

Leeward Hwy.

Grace Bay Rd.

The Saltmills

Port of Call

The Bight

Governor's Rd.

Casablanca
Casino

Provo Golf
Club

Leeward Hwy.

Long Bay Hwy.

Anacaona, **19**
Atlantic Bar & Grill, **1**
Bay Bistro, **9**
Bella Luna, **14**
Cabana Bar & Grill, **25**

Caicos Café, **21**
Calico Jack's, **16**
Coco Bistro, **24**
Coyaba Restaurant, **22**

Danny Buoy's
Irish Club, **13**
Fresh Bakery
& Bistro, **23**
Grace's Cottage, **10**

Grill Rouge at
Grace Bay Club, **20**
Jimmy's Dive Bar, **17**
LunaSea, **7**
Opus, **26**

The Orchid at
Alexandria Resort, **4**
O'Soleil, **8**
Parallel23, **5**
Pizza Pizza, **15**

The Plunge at
Regent Palms, **6**
Saltmills
Café & Diner, **11**
Seaside Café, **18**
Simba, **2**

Somewhere
on the Beach Café &
Lounge, **3**
Yoshi's Japanese
Restaurant, **16**

2

$$$–$$$$ ✕**Bay Bistro.** You simply can't eat any closer to the beach
⏱ than here, the only restaurant in all of Provo that is built
directly on the sand. Although service can be slow, the food
and setting are excellent. You dine on a covered porch sur-
rounded by palm trees and the sound of lapping waves.
The spring roll appetizer is excellent, and the oven-roasted
chicken is the best on the island. Junior, one of Provo's top
bartenders, might bring your drink balanced on the top of
his head. Brunch on weekends includes such favorites as
eggs Benedict with mimosas (included) and is very popular;
lines can be long if you don't have a reservation. ⊠*Sibonné,
Princess Dr., Grace Bay* ☎649/946–5396 ▤*AE, MC, V*
⊗*No dinner Mon.*

ROMANCE ON THE BEACH. What more romantic way to celebrate
a special occasion than with a terrific dinner directly on the
beach? Several Provo restaurants will set a table on the shore-
line, complete with tiki torches, candles, and tablecloths. Anaca-
ona, Bay Bistro, Orchid, O'Soleil, and Kissing Fish Catering are
a few of the places that will set up fantastic dinners. It's a great
setting for a marriage proposal.

$$$–$$$$ ✕**Bella Luna Ristorante.** For old-fashioned Italian food just
like you can get at home, where pasta is the side dish, this
is your best bet on Provo. The restaurant, which is a con-
verted private residence, offers a peaceful ambience. You
can also sit out in the gardens, which are threaded with lit
paths at night. Veal, fish, and chicken are made with fresh
herbs and wine-cream sauces, olive oil, and lemon butter.
The best dish on the menu is the chicken sautéed with red
peppers in a demi-glace flamed with cognac. If lobster Fra
Diavolo is not on the menu, ask for it. But be warned, it's
hot! ⊠ *Grace Bay Rd., Grace Bay* ☎649/946–5214 ▤*AE,
D, DC, MC, V* ⊗*Closed Sun. July–Sept. No lunch.*

$–$$ ✕**Cabana Bar & Grill.** Located at Ocean Club East, this is a
great option if you're looking for lunch with a view. The
food is good but unexciting, including such basic fare as
hamburgers and wraps. Here, it's about eating quickly then
getting go back to the beautiful beach just steps away.
Monday night happy hours make this a prime sunset-
watching spot. ⊠*Ocean Club East, Grace Bay Rd., Grace
Bay* ☎649/946–5880 ⬧ *Reservations not accepted* ▤*AE,
MC, V.*

$$$ ✕**Caicos Café.** There's an air of celebration on the tree-shaded terrace of this popular eatery. Choose from grilled seafood, steak, lamb, or chicken served hot off the outdoor barbecue. The sauces are French with a twist, often utilizing wine or cognac but with hot sauce added for Caribbean heat. Owner-chef Pierrik Marziou adds a French accent to his appetizers, salads, and homemade desserts, along with an outstanding collection of fine French wines. Wear bug spray at night. ⊠*Caicos Café Plaza, Grace Bay Rd., Grace Bay* ☎*649/946–5278* ⊟*AE, D, MC, V* ⊗*Closed Sun.*

$$ ✕**Calico Jack's Bar & Restaurant.** A great place to hang out, this is a top destination on Friday nights, when live bands play and there is dancing on the deck. The casual atmosphere offers a welcome break from Provo's upscale restaurants, both from dressing up and for your wallet. You'll find pasta night specials for $14 and typical bar appetizers such as wings and nachos. Burgers, pizza, and spaghetti please the kids, while grilled grouper or a juicy rib-eye steak pleases the adults. ⊠*Ports of Call Shopping Center, Grace Bay Rd., Grace Bay* ☎*649/946–5129* ⚠*Reservations not accepted* ⊟*AE, D, MC, V.*

$$$$ ✕**Coco Bistro.** With tables under palm trees, not only is the
★ setting divine, but the food is just as good. Though not directly on the beach, the location under the tropical tree grove still reminds you that you are on vacation. Main courses are complimented by both French flourishes (served au poivre, for example) and West Indian (such as with mango chutney) and are accompanied by fried plantains and mango slaw to maintain a Caribbean flair. Consider conch soup, soft-shell crab tempura, and sun-dried tomato pasta from the internationally influenced menu. This is one of the better restaurants on Provo. ⊠ *Grace Bay Rd., Grace Bay* ☎*649/946–5369* ⚠*Reservations essential* ⊟*AE, D, MC, V* ⊗*Closed Mon. No lunch.*

★ **Fodor's**Choice ✕**Coyaba Restaurant.** Directly behind Grace Bay
$$$$ Club and next to Caribbean Paradise Inn, this posh eatery serves nostalgic favorites with tempting twists in conversation-piece crockery and in a palm-fringed setting. Chef Paul Newman uses his culinary expertise for the daily-changing main courses, which includes exquisitely presented dishes such as crispy, whole yellow snapper fried in Thai spices. One standout is lobster thermidor in a Dijon-mushroom cream sauce. Try several different appetizers instead of one more expensive entrée for dinner; guava-

and-tamarind barbecue ribs and coconut shrimp tempura are two good choices if you go that route. If you enjoy creative menus, this is the place for you. Chef Paul keeps the resident expat crowd happy with traditional favorites like lemon meringue pie, albeit with his own tropical twist. Don't skip dessert; Paul makes the most incredible chocolate fondant you will ever have, and the service is seamless. ⊠*Off Grace Bay Rd., beside the Caribbean Paradise Inn, Grace Bay* ☎*649/946–5186* ⚷*Reservations essential* ▭*AE, MC, V* ⊘*Closed Tues. No lunch.*

2

$–$$ ✕**Danny Buoy's Irish Pub.** A true local watering hole, this bar always has a mix of locals and vacationers. It's your typical pub atmosphere, where you can watch your favorite sport no matter what part of the world you're from and dine on traditional Irish favorites such as fish-and-chips and potpies. Especially on weekends, this is one of the few places with some nightlife, and you will always find it open late. ⊠*Grace Bay Rd., Grace Bay* ☎*649/946–5921* ⚷*Reservations not accepted* ▭*AE, MC, V.*

$ ✕**Fresh Bakery & Bistro.** With the opening of this eatery across the street from Casablanca Casino, it's now easier to pack a picnic and explore. You can buy salads and deli sandwiches made with bread baked daily. Specials usually include ham and cheese puffs and shish kebab chicken with mashed potatoes, all packed to go. Don't forget to end with dessert; the European-style pastries are delectable. You can even call the order in first, so you can spend more time on the beach and less time waiting, but the bakery closes fairly early (at 6 PM most nights, 2 PM on Sunday). ⊠ *Grace Bay Rd., Grace Bay* ☎*649/345–4745* ▭*AE, MC, V* ⊘*No dinner.*

$$$$ ✕**Grace's Cottage.** At one of the prettiest dining settings on ★ Provo, tables are artfully set under wrought-iron cottage-style gazebos and around the wraparound veranda, which skirts the gingerbread-covered main building. In addition to such tangy and exciting entrées as panfried red snapper with roasted pepper sauce or melt-in-your-mouth grilled beef tenderloin with truffle-scented mashed potatoes, the soufflés are well worth the 15-minute wait and the top-tier price tag. Portions are small, but the quality is amazing. Service is impeccable (ladies are given a small stool so that their purses do not touch the ground). ⊠*Point Grace, Grace Bay* ☎*649/946–5096* ⚷*Reservations essential* ▭*D, MC, V* ⊘*No lunch.*

$$$–$$$$ ✕**Grill Rouge at Grace Bay Club.** Next to Anacaona, Grace Bay Club's premier restaurant, the Grill is the best option for families staying at the Club, since it allows children. The setting is gorgeous, with a wooden trellis, banquettes, and fire pits set in the sand under scattered awnings. The menu is more casual than that of Anacaona, with typical grill fare such as hamburgers and chicken and fish sandwiches; and it's also open for lunch. If you want something more substantial, you can order from Anacaona's menu. It's a good thing the setting is gorgeous, because service can be extremely slow. ✉ *Villas at Grace Bay Club, Grace Bay* ☎649/946–5050 ⊟*AE, D, MC, V.*

$$–$$$ ✕**Jimmy's Dive Bar.** A casual option that's not hard on the wallet, this restaurant is a terrific choice for breakfast in the Ports of Call shopping center. Expect mostly hamburgers and sandwiches, but if you're craving something more, you can get pasta, lobster (in season), and a huge 24-ounce porterhouse steak. It's in a great spot for people-watching, and it's open later than other restaurants, so if you're coming off a late flight, this is a good bet for food or just a lively spot to meet other vacationers. ✉*Ports of Call, Grace Bay Rd., Grace Bay* ☎649/946–5282 ⚓ *Reservations not accepted* ⊟*AE, D, DC, MC, V.*

$$ ✕**LunaSea.** At the Somerset Resort, in a gazebo with views of the gorgeous colors of Grace Bay Beach, you'll think you're truly having your burger in paradise. Other lunch offerings include hot dogs, fish-and-chips, and the outstanding chicken wrap with pecans and apples. Ask the chef if he's willing to make satay chicken with peanut sauce; it is the best lunch on the island. The bartender makes exotic tropical martinis, such as the mangotini, that you can sip by the pool. Recently, the bar has added buckets of beer that are brought to you on the beach so you never have to leave your little piece of paradise. ✉*The Somerset Resort, Princess Rd., Grace Bay* ☎649/946–5900 ⚓*Reservations not accepted* ⊟*AE, MC, V.*

$$$ ✕**Opus.** If you arrive in Provo on a late-evening flight, you still have a chance for fine dining. This is one of the few restaurants open until 11 PM. A beautifully landscaped patio is a quietly elegant setting. The menu here emphasizes meat: a fire-grilled rib-eye steak with cognac-cream sauce, filet mignon with horseradish demi-glace, and pork chops with salsa. If you want fish, order one of the daily specials. The best part of the meal is dessert; who can pass up the choco-

A Break from Restaurants

CLOSE UP

Provo offers some of the conveniences of home. There is one large supermarket, Graceway IGA, that has a full-service deli and bakery. It's a huge supermarket like you would find at home, with popular American, Canadian, and British brands. Prices are 25% to 50% more than what you would pay at home. The store also sells everything you need for the beach, from suntan lotion to beach chairs and floats. It is centrally located, so that if you get tired of eating out and spending lots of money, you will have a wonderful alternative.

There are also smaller markets such as Cost Right and Island Pride that offer similar products on a smaller scale. Graceway IGA will soon offer a gourmet market across from Seven Stars Resort, within walking distance of most resorts on Grace Bay Road. Some resorts have small convenience stores for staples such as milk, snacks, and coffee. The best places for ice are the supermarkets, as well as Gourmet Goods on Grace Bay Road. Most resorts offer a shuttle to IGA. Many villas and condos offer kitchens or kitchenettes, so you can eat at home.

late brownies with cheesecake swirl? Make sure to have a nightcap at the bar; it gets lively around 10. ✉ *Ocean Club East, Grace Bay Rd., Grace Bay* ☎ *649/946–5885* ⊟ *AE, D, DC, MC, V* ⊘ *No lunch.*

$$$ ✕**The Orchid at the Alexandra Resort.** A beautiful setting on a deck on the dunes offers endless views of Grace Bay. The restaurant is famous for its theme nights. Caribbean fare such as ribs with rice and peas is served up with karaoke on Monday; Mexican fare, including make-your-own tacos and burritos, is on the bill for Friday. This is one of the few restaurants in Provo that offers a buffet. On nontheme nights you can order casual food including conch fritters, grilled grouper, and jerk chicken pasta. Happy hour specials from 5:30 to 6:30 daily make this an excellent spot to watch the sunset. ✉ *Alexandra Resort, Princess Dr., Grace Bay* ☎ *649/946–5807 Ext. 7517* ⊟ *AE, MC, V.*

$$$ ✕**O'Soleil.** Located at the Somerset, this is one of Provo's
★ few indoor, air-conditioned restaurants, though you can also eat outside on the terrace. White-on-white decor under vaulted ceilings gives it a Miami-chic ambience. The executive chef mixes international styles, including influences from the Caribbean, Asia, and Europe. Some of the standouts include the best sea bass on the island served with

balsamic cherry tomatoes; roasted Australian rack of lamb; and excellent risotto. You can also order from of the tapas menu—the presentations are as creative as the food. Check out the conch spring rolls and shrimp tempura, each with its own dipping sauce. Eat on a couch under the stars during Friday night happy hour while listening to Daniel and Nadine sing the latest songs. Ask for simpler off-the-menu options for the children. ⊠ *The Somerset, Princess Dr., Grace Bay* ☎ *649/946–5900* ⊟ *AE, D, MC, V.*

$$$$ ×**Parallel 23.** The menu at the upscale dining room of the Regent Palms focuses primarily on fish and seafood. You sit outdoors on a covered porch looking into a courtyard, which may make you feel like you're dining on the porch of a majestic plantation. Two servers assigned to each table ensure good service. If only the food were as divine as the ambience, but it's just not consistent enough to justify these prices; meat can be overcooked. Some dishes have upscale, contemporary additions like truffle-infused fennel "foam" and shiitake chips, but most entrée sauces are heavy on the heat without enough flavor. ⊠ *Regent Palms Resort, Grace Bay* ☎ *649/946–8666* ⚓ *Reservations essential* ⊟ *AE, MC, V* ⊘ *No lunch.*

$$ ×**Pizza Pizza.** Sometimes you just don't want to dress up to go out. Sometimes, even on Provo, your wallet needs a vacation. Here is your answer. The menu includes all the standard toppings, including pepperoni, onions, green peppers, and olives, but there are also some more exotic options like conch, mussels, clams, and squid. In addition to good pizza, don't forget excellent lasagna; not only is it tasty, but you'll have enough left over for lunch the next day. You can either pick up your food or have it delivered so you can enjoy a balcony picnic. ⊠ *Grace Bay Plaza, Grace Bay Rd., Grace Bay* ☎ *649/941–8010* ⊟ *AE, D, DC, MC, V.*

$$–$$$ ×**The Plunge at Regent Palms.** This sunken restaurant by the pool offers a colorful and vibrant setting and is a great spot for people-watching. You can choose to sit in a long banquette with colorful pillows, at the bar, or on swim-up tables built right into the pool so you can eat in your swimsuit. The menu offers a break from the upscale Palms restaurant, with ribs, hamburgers, and pizza among the casual choices. But the best lunch choice is the chicken wrap with its creamy sauce. Be prepared to pay, though; even tea refills are charged individually. ⊠ *Regent Palms, Grace Bay* ☎ *649/946–8666* ⊟ *AE, D, DC, MC, V.*

$$ ✕**Saltmills Café & Diner.** This café has always been a favorite on Provo for breakfast, but the restaurant has expanded and now serves dinner, too. In a bright, multicolored 1950s-style diner you can get exactly what you would expect back home, everything from fish fingers to ribs to burgers. Relatively easy on the wallet, it's a fun family break from fine dining. ⊠*Saltmills Plaza, Grace Bay Rd., Grace Bay* ☎*649/941–8148* ♏*Reservations not accepted* ▭*AE, MC, V.*

$$$ ✕**Seaside Café.** The casual restaurant at Ocean Club West is a clone of the Cabana Bar & Grill at Ocean Club East. Usual lunch fare, such as hamburgers, salads, and wraps, can be eaten with a view of Grace Bay Beach. ⊠*Ocean Club West, Grace Bay Rd., Grace Bay* ☎*649/946–5880* ▭*AE, MC, V* ☻*No dinner.*

$$$ ✕**Simba.** Fishbowl-size glassware is all part of the charm ♺ at this larger-than-life, safari-themed poolside restaurant at the quieter end of Grace Bay. For the price, the Caribbean-inspired dishes with fruity twists like grouper with curry and mango sauce, conch with coconut curry, or salmon with tropical fruit salsa, are above expectations. A plus: this is one of just a few places with indoor, air-conditioned seating, but you need a car to get here (unless staying at the Turks & Caicos Club). ⊠*Turks & Caicos Club, West Grace Bay* ☎*649/946–5888* ♏*Reservations essential* ▭*AE, D, MC, V* ☻*No dinner Wed.*

$$ ✕**Somewhere on the Beach Café and Lounge.** Tex-Mex finally came to Grace Bay in 2009, but for now you can only have breakfast or lunch. One of the best breakfasts on the island is enhanced by great views. Try the breakfast burrito, a light tortilla filled with scrambled eggs, peppers, and homemade salsa. For lunch, the black bean salsa and homemade guacamole are the best anywhere. A three-tiered outdoor terrace is under construction at this writing and will make for terrific sunset dining. While the food is always good, if owner Carmen is cooking this is the best place to start your day. ⊠*Coral Gardens Resort, Lower Bight* ☎*649/245–2819* ▭*No credit cards* ☻*No dinner.*

$$–$$$ ✕**Yoshi's Japanese Restaurant.** It's amazing that you can get excellent Japanese food on a Caribbean island, and it's one of the few restaurants with indoor air-conditioned seating. The menu here is reasonably priced, and includes fresh sushi and basics like chicken teriyaki. The house salad with ginger dressing and the appetizer spring rolls are a delight.

Weekly Restaurant Happenings

CLOSE UP

Many of Provo's restaurants have weekly specials you can count on. Here are some of our favorites.

Wednesday nights are hopping at Tiki Hut, which has a $13 rib special. The restaurant only takes reservations for five or more people—so get there early and be prepared to wait. It's a popular night.

On Thursday nights at Hemingway's, Quentin Dean plays his Caribbean-accented versions of popular songs, offering an excellent opportunity for the kids to dance while you dine.

On Friday nights, start early at Da Conch Shack, where you dance right on the beach. Follow by going to Calico Jack's around 10 PM; it's great when the live bands make you feel like dancing on the deck.

By Saturday you may need to sleep in. But on Saturday night check out Nikki Beach for a pig roast in the sand.

Have a great Sunday brunch at Bay Bistro; it doesn't offer a traditional buffet, but the setting is great, and the included mimosas help too! In the afternoon head to the Blue Hills and Horse-Eyed Jack's for family day, where you can play beach volleyball, fly a kite, and listen to Quentin Dean play live music starting at around 4 PM. If you need more adult action, check out Nikki Beach's brunch, with interactive champagne parties and beautiful girls dancing on the pool bar.

If you don't want to stay indoors, it's a great place to sit outside and people-watch, too. ⊠ *Saltmills Plaza, Grace Bay Rd., Grace Bay* ☎649/941–3374 ⊟*AE, D, MC, V* ⊗*No lunch Sun.*

TURTLE COVE

¢–$ ✕**Angela's Top o' the Cove New York Style Delicatessen.** Order deli sandwiches, salads, enticingly rich desserts, and freshly baked pastries at this island institution on Leeward Highway, just south of Turtle Cove. From the deli case you can buy the fixings for a picnic; the shelves are stocked with an eclectic selection of fancy foodstuffs, as well as beer and wine. It's open at 6:30 AM for a busy trade in coffees, cappuccinos, and frappaccinos. This is the best cheese steak you'll ever have outside Philly, but the location isn't where most tourists stay—it's worth the drive, though. ⊠*Leeward Hwy., Turtle Cove* ☎649/946–4694 ⊟*AE, MC, V* ⊗*No dinner.*

2

$$-$$$ ✕**Aqua Bar & Terrace.** This popular restaurant on the grounds
⏱ of the Turtle Cove Inn has an inviting waterfront dining
deck, and it just keeps getting better. The menu leans heavily toward locally caught seafood and farm-raised conch,
and includes longtime favorites like Wahoo sushi, pecan-
encrusted conch fillets, and grilled fish served with flavorful
sauces. A selection of more casual entrées, including salads
and burgers, appeals to the budget-conscious. There are
plenty of child-friendly menu options. Bring bug spray, as
you're close to the water. ⊠*Turtle Cove Inn, Turtle Cove
Marina, Turtle Cove* ☎*649/946–4763* ⊟*AE, MC, V.*

$$-$$$ ✕**Baci Ristorante.** Aromas redolent of the Mediterranean
waft from the open kitchen as you enter this intimate eatery
east of Turtle Cove. Outdoor seating is on a romantic
canal-front patio, one of the lovelier settings on Provo. The
menu offers a small but varied selection of Italian dishes.
Veal is prominent on the menu, but main courses also
include pasta, chicken, fish, and brick-oven pizzas. You'll
never see redder tomatoes than those in the tomato and
mozzarella Caprese salad; a standout entrée is the chicken
with vodka-cream sauce. House wines are personally
selected by the owners and complement the tasteful wine
list. Try tiramisu for dessert with a flavored coffee drink.
Wear bug spray at night. ⊠*Harbour Town, Turtle Cove*
☎*649/941–3044* ⊟*AE, MC, V.*

$$$ ✕**Magnolia Wine Bar & Restaurant.** Restaurateurs since the
★ early 1990s, hands-on owners Gianni and Tracey Capor-
uscio make success seem simple. Expect well-prepared,
uncomplicated choices that range from European to Asian
to Caribbean. You can construct an excellent meal from
the outstanding appetizers; do not miss the spring rolls and
the grilled-vegetable-and-fresh-mozzarella stack; finish your
meal with the mouthwatering molten chocolate cake. The
atmosphere is romantic, the presentations attractive, and
the service careful. It's easy to see why the Caporuscios
have a loyal following. The adjoining wine bar includes a
handpicked list of specialty wines, which can be ordered
by the glass. The marine setting is a great place to watch
the sunset. ⊠*Miramar Resort, Turtle Cove* ☎*649/941–
5108* ⊟*AE, D, MC, V* ⊙*Closed Mon. No lunch.*

$$ ✕**Sharkbites Bar & Grill.** A local favorite with a huge deck
over the water overlooks Turtle Cove Marina. The standard
fare incorporates everything from the local catch in sandwiches to nachos and beer. It's a casual place for lunch,

and during the day sometimes sharks will swim around the deck—exciting for kids and a good destination if you don't want to do fine dining for dinner. Friday-night happy hour makes this a popular place to meet locals. ⊠*Turtle Cove Marina, Turtle Cove* ☎649/941–5090 ⚓*Reservations not accepted* ▭*AE, D, MC, V.*

$$ ✕**Tiki Hut.** From its location overlooking the marina, the
☺ ever-popular Tiki Hut continues to serve consistently tasty, value-priced meals in a fun atmosphere. Locals take advantage of the Wednesday-night $13 chicken-and-rib special, and the lively bar is a good place to sample local Turks Head brew. There's a special family-style menu (the best kid's menu in Provo) and kids' seating. Don't miss pizzas made with the signature white sauce; or the jerk wings coated in a secret barbecue sauce then grilled—they're out of this world! The restaurant can be busy, with long waits for a table, and you can only reserve with five people or more. Just added: Daniel and Nadine will sing while you dine on Sunday nights. ⊠*Turtle Cove Marina, Turtle Cove* ☎649/941–5341 ▭*AE, D, MC, V.*

ELSEWHERE ON PROVIDENCIALES

$ ✕**Corner Café.** The perfect stop for a quick breakfast or lunch or even early light dinner, its location next to the supermarket makes it a convenient stop. There is a sandwich on the menu that will suit almost any taste, with honey ham, prosciutto, chicken salad, and even salmon among the choices. Each is made to order with bread that's baked fresh daily. This is also a great choice for your caffeine rush; you can choose coffee, cappuccino, or espresso. ⊠*Leeward Hwy., next to Graceway IGA, Discovery Bay* ☎649/941–8724 ▭*No credit cards* ☉*Closed Sun.*

$–$$ ✕**Da Conch Shack.** An institution in Provo for many years, this brightly colored beach shack is justifiably famous for its conch and seafood. The legendary specialty, conch, is fished fresh out of the shallows and either cooked, spiced, cracked, or fried to absolute perfection. On Friday nights you can dance in the sand after dinner. This is freshest conch anywhere on the island, as the staff dive for it only after you've placed your order, but if you don't like seafood, there is chicken on the menu. Thursday nights start rocking while you eat and mingle with the locals; Daniel and Nadine have just been added as headliners to sing songs that make everybody happy. ⊠*Blue Hills Rd., Blue Hills* ☎ *No phone* ⊟*No credit cards* ⊙*No lunch.*

$-$$ ✕**Hole in the Wall.** Off the beaten path, this is a spot where mostly locals hang out. The menu is heavy on the fresh catch of the day, but the restaurant also offers visitors the opportunity to get a taste of local cuisine such as oxtail and curried goat. A typical Caribbean breakfast here consists of saltfish or liver and onions with grits. For picky eaters, there are also chicken, ribs, and pork chops on the menu. ⊠ *Williams Plaza, Old Airport Rd., Airport* ☎649/941–4136 ⚓ *Reservations not accepted* ⊟*No credit cards.*

$$-$$$ ✕**Las Brisas Restaurant & Bar.** With exquisite views of Chalk Sound, the setting here is perfect. An outdoor deck and gazebo offer picture-postcard views of the neon-turquoise water of Chalk Sound that must be seen to be believed. The only restaurant on Provo that focuses on Spanish cuisine offers an excellent paella. The menu also includes tapas, so you can nibble for lunch while you gaze at the gorgeous water. Dinner takes a little longer, as everything is made to order; you pick out your fish or meat, decide how you want it prepared, and choose a sauce for it. If the reasonable prices weren't enough for a visit, the views alone are worth it. ⊠*Neptune Villas, Chalk Sound Rd., Chalk Sound* ☎649/342–0138 ⊟*AE MC, V.*

$$-$$$ ✕**Matsuri Sushi Bar.** Located next to the Graceway IGA supermarket, this little sushi bar offers incredible sushi that almost makes you forget you're in a British colony. Fresh ingredients and air-conditioned indoor seating will help you satisfy your Japanese cravings. More offerings on the extensive menu include teriyaki chicken and Wagyu beef, along with miso soup and salads with ginger dressing. ⊠*Leeward Hwy., Discovery Bay* ☎649/941–3274 ⊟*AE, MC, V.*

$$$$ ✕**The Restaurant at Amanyara.** While this restaurant doesn't have an official name, that small omission shouldn't keep you from dining here. The setting, around pavilions with pools, is completely unique on Provo. Some tables are by the beach with ocean breezes, others are indoors with air-conditioning. Bring bug spray at dusk if dining outside— you are surrounded by water. For guests of the resort, the restaurant is the only choice for dinner, unless you take a long and expensive taxi ride to other restaurants. If you are not an Amanyara guest, make reservations at least two days in advance for either lunch or dinner, if you can get them at all. It will be worth the effort; the food is fantastic, with the freshest seafood and choicest cuts of meat available in Provo. The menu changes daily, but always includes a choice of fish, meat, chicken, or lamb. The sauces have an Asian flair, with soy-infused wine reduction on the steaks and vegetable-fried rice for a side. Meat lovers will find the best steak on the island here. ⊠ *Amanyara Resort, Malcolm's Beach* ☎ *649/941–8133* ⚓ *Reservations essential* ▭ *AE, MC, V.*

$$–$$$ ✕ **Sailing Paradise.** This restaurant frequented by locals is a great place to watch the regulars play "slamming" dominos. The food is local, too. Breakfast is typical Caribbean fare such as fish, grits, and rice and peas. Lunch and dinner consist of the daily local catch; the beer is Turks Head or Jamaican Red Stripe. What sets this restaurant apart from the others is the colorful atmosphere—little huts all painted in different hues, with a huge deck so you can watch the fishermen come in with their catch while you eat. The buildings are a photographer's delight; they have even been used as the backdrop by the Tourism Department for all of its international ad campaigns. ⊠ *Blue Hills Rd., Blue Hills* ☎ *649/941–7485* ⚓ *Reservations not accepted* ▭ *No credit cards.*

$$ ✕ **Smokey's on Da Bay.** People flock to Smokey's for fantastic ribs and authentic rice and peas, making it one of the best local places to eat. In Blue Hills, it's little more than a simple Caribbean eating shack on the beach, with men slamming dominoes and a Wednesday-night fish fry. ⊠ *Blue Hills Rd., Blue Hills* ☎ *649/941–7852* ▭ *No credit cards.*

WHERE TO STAY

It's rare to find a truly bad place to stay on Providenciales. Most of the hotels, resorts, and villas on Provo are impeccably maintained; all are clean and comfortable, and most offer up-to-date, modern conveniences such as air-conditioning, satellite TV, and Wi-Fi. Since Provo is relatively new to the tourism business, most resorts are just a few years old. The majority of accommodations are individually owned condos placed in a rental pool and treated as a resort. You get the best of both worlds in these condo resorts: luxurious, full living areas that come with resort amenities such as toiletries, excursion desks, and towels for the beach. Except for the Comfort Suites, Club Med, and Beaches resorts, you won't find any chains represented. Even the island's more basic accommodations are nice, with comfortable rooms with all the expected conveniences. More upscale accommodations offer pure luxury; most have full kitchens, state-of-the-art appliances, and lavish furnishings—some are probably nicer than the house you live in. The resorts offer various levels of services and run the gamut from straightforward condo complexes without restaurants or excursion desks to full-service resorts with room service and pampering on the beach. Almost all the hotels and resorts are located in the Grace Bay area, sometimes referred as Provo's "Golden Mile"; there are only a few hotels located in Turtle Cove, Northwest Point, and Chalk Sound.

Provo is one of the better islands in the Caribbean for renting a private villa; there are a plethora to choose from that offer a clean, comfortable home away from home. Villas are scattered across the island, so you can choose whether you want to be close to activity or have peace and quiet. Villas range from romantic one-bedroom homes on the beach to fantastic multibedroom mansions on private stretches of sand, with everything in between. If you do stay in a villa, then you'll need to rent a car, sometimes just to get to the beach. Most villas are in areas that are not close to restaurants. Some can be found in residential neighborhoods, such as Leeward, where homes may be on a canal or a couple of blocks from the beach. Several villas are in quiet Turtle Tail, conveniently located behind the Graceway IGA supermarket. These offer views of the stunning Caicos Banks. The villas around Sapodilla Bay, Taylor Bay, and Chalk Sound usually have gorgeous views in all directions. A villa can offer a more budget-friendly vacation if you split the costs with other couples or families.

WHAT IT COSTS

$$$$	$$$	$$	$	¢
HOTELS*				
over $350	$250–$350	$150–$250	$80–$150	under $80
HOTELS**				
over $450	$350–$450	$250–$350	$125–$250	under $125

*EP, BP, CP **AI, FAP, MAP
Restaurant prices are for a main course at dinner and include any taxes or service charges. Hotel prices are per night for a double room in high season, excluding taxes, service charges, and meal plans (except at all-inclusives).

HOTELS AND RESORTS

Most resorts on Provo are composed of privately owned condos that are placed into the resort's rental pool when the owners are not present. Unlike at chain hotels and resorts, you cannot request a particular building, floor, or room unless you are a repeat visitor. If you fall in love with the condo, you can probably purchase it or one that's similar. There are no taxes in Turks and Caicos except for a onetime stamp-duty tax—no property tax and no rental tax—which makes owning your own piece of paradise even more tempting.

GRACE BAY

The vast majority of the hotels and resorts on Providenciales have been developed along beautiful Grace Bay, between the Turtle Cove Marina on the west and Leeward on the east.

$$$–$$$$ ⊡**The Alexandra Resort.** All the comfortable, spacious rooms ☾ at this beachfront condo resort have some type of ocean or pool view—no parking-lot views here. Appointments are decidedly upscale: granite countertops, stainless-steel appliances, a washer and dryer, and feather-top pillows on the beds. The friendliest staff on the island will make you feel like family. At this writing there is some construction underway, which has prompted the management to offer specials, and these can be some of the best deals on Provo. **Pros:** luxury for less; all rooms have ocean views. **Cons:** lots of construction in the vicinity; temporary reception gives a bad first impression; while most resorts have king beds, this one has only queens. ⊠*Princess Dr., Grace Bay* ☎*649/946–5807 or 800/704–9424* ⊕*www.alexandraresort.com* ⬐*88 rooms* ☍*In-room: safe, kitchen (some), DVD, Wi-Fi. In-hotel: restaurant, bar, tennis courts, pool, gym, beachfront, water sports, laundry facilities* ⊟*AE, D, MC, V* ⍩*EP.*

$$$$ ⊡**Beaches Turks & Caicos Resort & Spa.** The largest resort in ☾ the Turks and Caicos Islands can satisfy families as eager ★ to spend time apart as together. Younger children and teenagers will appreciate a children's park, complete with video-game center, waterslides, a swim-up soda bar, and even a teen disco. Parents may prefer the extensive spa, pretty beach, and complimentary scuba diving. Rooms, suites, and cottage villas are decorated in standard tropical themes, but the resort's major draw is found outside the rooms, where there are numerous activities and a choice

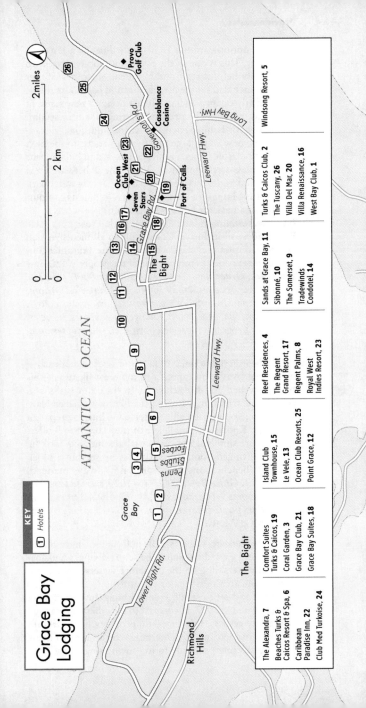

Grace Bay Lodging

KEY
⬜1 Hotels

Richmond
Hills

Lower Bight Rd.

ATLANTIC OCEAN

Grace
Bay

Penns
Stubbs
Forbes

Grace Bay Rd.

The Bight

Leeward Hwy.

Ocean Club West

Seven Stars

Port of Calls

Governor's Rd.

Casablanca Casino

◆ Provo Golf Club

Leeward Hwy.

Long Bay Hwy.

N

2miles

2 km

The Alexandra, **7**
Beaches Turks &
Caicos Resort & Spa, **6**
Caribbean
Paradise Inn, **22**
Club Med Turkoise, **24**

Comfort Suites
Turks & Caicos, **19**
Coral Garden, **3**
Grace Bay Club, **21**
Grace Bay Suites, **18**

Island Club
Townhouse, **15**
Le Vele, **13**
Ocean Club Resorts, **25**
Point Grace, **12**

Reef Residences, **4**
The Regent
Grand Resort, **17**
Regent Palms, **8**
Royal West
Indies Resort, **23**

Sands at Grace Bay, **11**
Sibonné, **10**
The Somerset, **9**
Tradewinds
Condotel, **14**

Turks & Caicos Club, **2**
The Tuscany, **26**
Villa Del Mar, **20**
Villa Renaissance, **16**
West Bay Club, **1**

Windsong Resort, **5**

of dining options, from a 1950s-style diner to a Japanese restaurant. This is one of the company's top resorts, with a generally helpful staff and excellent amenities. Butler service is included for the presidential and penthouse suites. The recently opened Italian Village brings a new sense of luxury to this sprawling resort, offering all-suites accommodations for families, new pools, and additional restaurants. The new suites take this Beaches resort to the next level, with marble floors, granite counters, and full kitchens with stainless-steel appliances. Built-in bunk beds are great for kids, and butler service helps parents. A new water park is one of the largest in the Caribbean. Nonguests can purchase a day pass for $140 per person to get access to all facilities, restaurants, and the water park. **Pros:** great place for families; all-inclusive. **Cons:** with an all-inclusive plan you miss out on the island's other great restaurants; construction next door to the east side of the property. ⊠*Lower Bight Rd., Grace Bay* ☎*649/946–8000 or 800/726–3257* ⊕*www.beaches.com* ⬐*359 rooms, 103 suites* &*In-room: safe, Internet. In-hotel: 9 restaurants, bars, tennis courts, pools, gym, spa, beachfront, diving, water sports, bicycles, children's programs (ages newborn–12), Internet terminal* ⊟*AE, MC, V* ⊺⊙*AI.*

$$ 🗆**Caribbean Paradise Inn.** Not far from Grace Bay Beach— but tucked away inland about a 10-minute walk away—this two-story bed-and-breakfast has terra-cotta walls and cobalt-blue trimmings. If you get to know manager Jean-Luc Bohic, you may be able to persuade him to prepare a barbecue. Rooms are smaller than the usual Provo offerings and are simply decorated with balconies overlooking the palm-fringed pool. **Pros:** pay less by staying a block from the beach. **Cons:** front desk not always manned. ⬀*Box 673, Grace Bay* ☎*649/946–5020* ⊕*www.paradise. tc* ⬐*16 rooms* &*In-room: safe, Wi-Fi, kitchen (some). In-hotel: bar, pool, Internet terminal, no-smoking rooms* ⊟*AE, MC, V* ⊺⊙*CP.*

$$$ 🗆**Club Med Turkoise.** Guests still fly in from the United States, Europe, and Canada to enjoy the scuba diving, windsurfing, and waterskiing on the turquoise waters at the doorsteps of the area's first major resort. Rooms in the village are basic and set in small, colorful bungalows that were last renovated in 2007. In contrast to the otherwise tranquil Grace Bay resorts, this energetic property has a vibrant party atmosphere, nightly entertainment, and even a flying trapeze, catering primarily to fun-loving singles and cou-

Crazy for Conch

CLOSE UP

Belongers, who are descended from the first slaves from Africa and Bermuda that settled the islands in the 1600s, know that the most important thing on their islands is also their biggest export: conch. They take full advantage of every part of the conch, from shell to meat. Every restaurant in the Turks and Caicos serves some type of conch, either in a sandwich, salad, fritter, soup, or even sushi. So loved is the conch that now it's used for other things, too. Shells are sold to tourists, who may bring back two shells per person. The pink part of the shell is used for homemade jewelry, especially bracelets and earrings. Shells are crushed and used at the Regent Palms Spa to exfoliate your skin.

Diving for conch has been incorporated into day trips. A local called Conch Man carves the shells into shapes like palm trees and other tropical objects. You can buy his creations in the Silverdeep boutique. Conch is embedded on the ledges of walls built around homes in Salt Cay, not only for a tropical look but also to keep cows and donkeys out of the yard.

The Conch Farm is the only commercial conch farm in the world, and a visit will show you how conch is grown and give you information about its many uses. You'll meet Sally and Jerry, two resident conchs who come out on cue. The farm was badly damaged during Hurricane Ike in 2008, but it is being rebuilt at this writing.

---

ples. **Pros:** all-inclusive; active. **Cons:** although the rooms have been updated, the grounds are showing their age. ✉*Grace Bay* ☎*649/946–5500 or 888/932–2582* ⊕*www. clubmed.com* ↩*293 rooms* ☆*In-room: Refrigerator. In-hotel: 3 restaurants, bars, tennis courts, pool, gym, spa, beachfront, diving, water sports, bicycles, laundry service, Internet terminal, Wi-Di, parking (fee), no kids under 18* ▭*AE, D, MC, V* ⦿*AI.*

$$ ▣**Comfort Suites Turks & Caicos.** At this writing one of only three chain properties in the Turks and Caicos, the Comfort Suites offers an acceptable alternative to some of Provo's higher-priced resorts. The colorful coral-colored building with a green tin roof is surrounded by lush flowers and palms around the pool. The rooms are quite large, and all have pull-out sleeper sofas and mini-refrigerators. The colors from the outside carry over inside, with green-wood furniture and light coral walls with tropical, multicolor linens. The pool bar is popular with locals, especially cab

drivers, who stop by to catch up on the gossip of the island. The hotel is across the street from the beach. You can get beach towels at the front desk, and the hotel sets up a couple of beach umbrellas too. The continental breakfast is just enough to hold you until lunch, consisting of coffee, orange juice, toast, and corn bread. The location is convenient, and you can easily walk to several of the island's less expensive restaurants in the Ports of Call shopping center. **Pros:** helps you stick to a budget; you know what to expect from a chain hotel; convenient location. **Cons:** you need to keep the room key in a slot for electricity; furniture not great despite a recent renovation; not directly on the beach. ⊠*Grace Bay Rd., Grace Bay* ☎*649/946–8888* ⊕*www. ComfortSuitesTCI.com* ⟳*100 suites* ♿*In-room: safe, refrigerator, Wi-Fi. In-hotel: bar, pool, Wi-Fi, parking (free), no-smoking rooms* ⊟*AE, D, DC, MC, V* ⊙*CP.*

$$$–$$$$ 🖼**Coral Gardens.** Some of the best off-the-beach snorkeling makes this location hard to resist; the best reef is the backyard. The units are huge, with sliding windows that, when open, make you feel as if you are almost outside. It has a weathered appearance and could use a coat of paint, but the units are completely adequate. Rooms have bamboo and wicker furnishings, with tropical prints and plush couches and beds. Two management companies share responsibility for the units here (separate Web sites, check-in, and even available amenities), so be sure you know who you are renting from. (The eight units managed by Reef Residences are reviewed separately.) The management of Coral Gardens is answerable to the majority of condo owners and manages the reception and the excellent dive shop Cactus Voyagers. Because of the dual management, prices for similar units may differ. **Pros:** resort fronts one of the best off-the-beach snorkeling spots on Provo; spacious rooms all have ocean views. **Cons:** maintenance is suffering; feuding management makes it unclear which amenities you are allowed to use. ⊠*Penn's Rd., Box 281, The Bight* ☎*649/941–5497 Coral Gardens on Grace Bay, 877/746–7800, 649/941–3713* ⊕*www.CoralGardenson-GraceBay.com* ⟳*54 suites* ♿*In-room: safe, kitchen, Wi-Fi. In-hotel: restaurant, bars, pools, spa, beachfront, diving, water sports, laundry facilities, Internet terminal, Wi-Fi* ⊟*AE, MC, V* ⊙*BP.*

$$$$ 🖼**Grace Bay Club, Villas at Grace Bay Club & the Estate at Grace**
☾ **Bay Club.** This small and stylish resort retains a loyal follow-
★ ing because of its helpful, attentive staff and unpretentious

CLOSE UP

What Is a Potcake?

Potcakes are indigenous dogs of the Bahamas and Turks and Caicos islands. Traditionally, these strays would be fed leftovers from the bottom of the pot, hence the name. Much is being done today to control the stray-dog population. The TCSPCA and Potcake Place are two agencies working to find homes for the puppies. You can do a good deed by adopting one of these gorgeous pups; they have received all the shots and have all the paperwork required to bring them into the United States. Even if you don't adopt, you can help by volunteering to bring one back to its adopted family. Clearing customs in the United States is actually easier when you bring back a potcake! For more information on how you can help, check out the Web site for Potcake Place (⊕ *www.potcakeplace.com*).

elegance. The architecture is reminiscent of Florence, with terra-cotta rooftops and a shaded courtyard, complete with fountain. Suites, all with sweeping sea views, have earthy tiles, luxurious white Egyptian cotton–covered beds, and Elemis toiletries. The ground-floor suites, fronted by large arched patios and lush azaleas, have a palatial feel and turquoise water views. New, ultraluxurious villas offer families a Grace Bay experience with a large pool, a bar and grill, and an impressive range of children's activities, including a bouncy castle in Kids Town, kayaking trips, and all sorts of "edutainment" to keep even teenagers occupied—and cookies, of course. Opened in January 2009, the Estate at Grace Bay Club has elevated this luxurious resort to a new level of privacy and elegance; ground-floor suites are extra spacious, and some have plunge pools. Estate at Grace Bay Club has a private restaurant, bar, and pool only for its guests. If you want a VIP feel, this is the place for you. **Pros:** gorgeous pool and restaurant lounge areas with outdoor couches, daybeds, and fire pits; all guests receive a cell phone to use on the island. **Cons:** no children allowed at Anacaona restaurant; construction in front of the properties. ⊠ *Grace Bay Rd., behind Grace Bay Court, Grace Bay* ☎*649/946–5050 or 800/946–5757* ⊕*www.gracebayclub.com* ⌖*59 suites* ☖*In-room: safe, kitchen, Internet, Wi-Fi. In-hotel: 2 restaurants, room service, bar, tennis courts, pools, spa, beachfront, water sports, bicycles, laundry facilities, laundry service, Internet terminal, Wi-Fi, no children under 12 (some)* ▭*AE, D, MC, V* ⍾*CP.*

$$ ⛶ **Grace Bay Suites.** A bargain compared to most hotels in the Grace Bay area, this hotel gives you your money's worth. The beach is an easy one-block walk. In the rooms, plush pillow-top mattresses and plasma TVs help you forget you got a bargain. Sharing the same management as Danny Buoy's Irish Pub *(see Where to Eat)* means you can have food delivered to the pool or to your room late at night, and each suite has a kitchenette. A central location behind Salt-mills Plaza and across the street from Regent Village allows easy access to shops and numerous restaurants, including entertainment. **Pros:** central location; a little luxury for less money; room service until late. **Cons:** no views; you're a block from the beach; no stove in kitchenette, which makes real cooking difficult. ⊠*Grace Bay Rd., Grace Bay* ☎*649/941–7447* ⊕*www.GraceBaySuites.com* ⇆*18 studios, 6 1 bedrooms* ⚿*In-room: safe, refrigerator, Internet, Wi-Fi. In-hotel: restaurant, room service, bar, pool, Wi-Fi, parking (free), no-smoking rooms* ⊟*AE, MC, V* |⚪|*EP.*

$ ⛶ **Island Club Townhouses.** Long-term renters usually live here, but if you're on a budget you won't find a place that gives you more for your money than this small condo complex. Island Club, next door to Saltmills Plaza, is in the heart of Grace Bay and just across the street from the beach. Three units are usually reserved for vacation rentals, and these town houses have everything you need at a terrific price. For only $900 a week you get a two-story, two-bedroom townhouse decorated with bamboo furniture, two bathrooms, a full kitchen, and a landscaped pool. And you get extras even at this price, including satellite TV and air-conditioning. On an island where most vacationers consider everything expensive, you can still vacation on a budget—a serious budget. With the full kitchen, you can shop for groceries and save on food; you are already saving on your hotel. The office provides beach towels and will lend you umbrellas to take to the beach. Island Club proves that you don't have to give up clean and comfortable rooms to save money in Provo. **Pros:** you can't get a better deal in Provo; centrally located so you can walk everywhere. **Cons:** the few condos for short-term rental go fast; no phones in the room; a block from the beach. ⊠*Grace Bay Rd., Grace Bay* ☎*649/946–5866* ⊕*www.IslandClubGrace-Bay.com* ⇆*24 2-bedroom apartments* ⚿*In-room: no phone, kitchen, DVD, Wi-Fi. In-hotel: pool, laundry facilities, Wi-Fi, parking (free), no-smoking rooms* ⚷*1 week minimum* ⊟*MC, V* |⚪|*EP.*

2

$$$$ ⌂**Le Vele.** Modern and chic, this condo resort looks as if it were transported directly from Miami's South Beach, minus the crowds. The furnishings are surprising, featuring plush couches and soothing calm colors such as green and turquoise. All the suites are oceanfront, and all have oversized balconies or patios to take advantage of the views and setting. Although there is no restaurant, the rates include a continental breakfast delivered to your room. The suites have everything needed for the independent traveler, including full kitchens, except the studios, which have a kitchenette with microwave and mini-refrigerator; all units have a washer and dryer. **Pros:** great central location; spacious rooms maximize the ocean views. **Cons:** more residential feel than hotel; modern buildings, though beautiful, don't blend with other resorts on the beach. ⊠*Grace Bay* ☎*649/941–8800* ⊕*www.LeVele.tc* ⇆*12 suites* ⌂*In-room: kitchen, DVD, Wi-Fi, Internet. In-hotel: pool, gym, Wi-Fi, Internet terminal, some pets allowed, parking (no fee)* ⊟*AE, D, DC, MC, V CP.*

$$$–$$$$ **Ocean Club Resorts.** Enormous, locally painted pictures of
☾ hibiscus make a striking first impression as you enter the
★ reception area at one of the island's mostestablished condominium resorts. Regular shuttles run along the ½-mi (1-km) stretch of Grace Bay Beach between two artfully landscaped properties, Ocean Club East and Ocean Club West, from 6 AM to 10:30 PM. Both resorts claim some of Provo's best amenities. Ocean Club East has the advantage of a quieter location away from most of the development and is just a short walk from Provo Golf & Country Club. Ocean Club West has a larger pool with a swim-up bar. Management and service are superb, as are the special-value packages offered most of the year. Plenty of beach and pool toys make Ocean Club East a good family option. **Pros:** family-friendly resort with shuttles between the two shared properties; screened balconies and porches allow a respite from incessant air-conditioning. **Cons:** both resorts are showing their age. ⌂*Box 240, Grace Bay* ☎*649/946–5880 or 800/457–8787* ⊕*www.oceanclubresorts.com* ⇆*174 suites: 86 at Ocean Club, 88 at Ocean Club West* ⌂*In-room: safe, kitchen (some). In-hotel: 2 restaurants, bars, tennis court, pools, gym, spa, beachfront, diving, water sports, laundry facilities, Internet terminal, Wi-Fi* ⊟*AE, D, MC, V* ⚘*EP.*

$$$$ ⌂**Point Grace.** Provo's answer to Parrot Cay has attracted celebrity guests, including Donatella Versace. Asian-influ-

Buying in Paradise

So what happens when you get your first glance of Grace Bay Beach, and you just have to own your own little piece of paradise? Well, the Turks and Caicos islands make it easy for you. Almost everything seems to be for sale here; chances are the condo where you're staying is for sale or that there's another just like it on the market. Adding to the temptation is that there is only a onetime stamp-duty tax paid during the transfer of land. Currently Provo charges 9.75%, although half-off tax specials have been known to happen. On the outer islands the tax is even less, from 3% to 5%. After you pay the stamp-duty tax, you never have to pay property taxes again, even if you rent out your unit.

Many people come down on vacation, fall in love with the beach, and buy property before thinking it through. As tempting as it may be, it's also important to be smart. Ask yourself the following: Can I rent this on my own, or do I have to put it in the management pool? What are the costs of maintenance, hurricane insurance, bug spraying, and travel-agent fees? What is the rental split with the management company? Can the resort decide to upgrade or make changes and send me the bill?

The best advice anyone can give is that you should buy a place because you love it, not just for the investment. The investment potential amounts to possible capital gains; in other words, you only make money when you resell your property for a profit. One final piece of advice: remember that you're placing your money in a foreign country, so always hire a local lawyer.

---

enced rooftop domes blend with Romanesque stone pillars and wide stairways in this plush resort, which offers spacious beachfront suites and romantic cottages surrounding the centerpiece: a turquoise infinity pool with perfect views of the beach. Antique furnishings, four-poster beds, and art reproductions give a classic style to the rooms. The second-story cottage suites are especially romantic. Bleached-wood cottages, on the sand dune, house a thalassotherapy spa presided over by elegant French spa manager Edmonde Sidibé. Other highlights include the restaurants, particularly the beautiful Grace's Cottage. Honeymooners can arrange a transfer in an authentic London taxi. **Pros:** relaxing environment; beautiful pool. **Cons:** can be stuffy (signs around the pool remind you to be quiet). ☎ *Box 700,*

Grace Bay ☎649/946–5096 or 888/924–7223 ⊕*www. pointgrace.com* ⇨*23 suites, 9 cottage suites, 2 villas* ⟁*In-room: safe, kitchen. In-hotel: 2 restaurants, room service, bars, pool, spa, beachfront, water sports, bicycles, laundry service, Internet terminal, no-smoking rooms* ⊟*AE, D, MC, V* ⊘*Closed Sept.* ⦿|*CP.*

$$$$ ⬚**Reef Residences.** Staying in a location that is not directly on Grace Bay Beach does not mean you must sacrifice luxury. Beautiful suites with colonial-style furnishings, granite countertops, and stainless-steel appliances make your stay comfortable. A path through Coral Gardens Resort leads to the restaurant owned by the management team of Reef Residences for your included breakfast, and this is also the way to the beach (Reef Residences sits behind Windsong Resort). At this writing Reef Residences also manages eight units at Coral Gardens; these units have different amenities than other Coral Gardens units, including breakfast and a half-hour massage, and are administered from the Reef Residences reception area, so make sure you know who you are renting from. While the location is nice, feuding management with neighboring Coral Gardens makes it hard to recommend. The restaurant reopened after being damaged by Hurricane Ike, and is now called Somewhere on The Beach, and offers a unique Tex-Mex breakfast. **Pros:** nice pool; spacious rooms. **Cons:** you have to walk through another resort to get to the beach; management of Reef Residences is feuding with the management at Coral Gardens, so service can be spotty at best. ⊠*Stubbs Rd., Lower Bight* ☎649/941–3713 ⊕*www.ReefResidence. com* ⇨*24 suites at Reef Residences, 8 suites at Coral Gardens* ⟁*In-room: safe, kitchen, DVD, Wi-Fi. In-hotel: restaurant, room service, bar, pools, gym, spa, parking (free), no-smoking rooms* ⊟*AE, MC, V* ⦿|*BP.*

$$$$ ⬚**The Regent Grand Resort.** Even bigger and more luxurious than its sister property, Villa Renaissance, the Regent Grand is centered on a courtyard with a four-leaf-clover-shaped pool that allows guests to get peace and quiet in a gorgeous setting. Italianate arches, trellises, and giant columns bring a distinct elegance. The rooms are colorful and comfortable, with colonial-style furnishings; all have huge patios or balconies facing Grace Bay Beach or the beautiful pool. While there is no restaurant on-site, it's an easy walk to numerous restaurants and shops in the Regent Village (on the resort property but not at the Regent Grand itself) and Saltmills shopping center. Another nearby property is under development. Regent Grand guests have golf privileges at the Provo Golf Course, where greens fees are discounted. **Pros:** majestic architecture with huge columns and arches; central location in walking distance of numerous restaurants and shops; upscale Regent Village shops nearby. **Cons:** no restaurant at the resort. ⊠*Regent St., Grace Bay* ☎*649/941–7770* ⊕*www.TheRegentGrandResort.com* ⇋*21 suites* ⌂*In-room: safe, kitchen, refrigerator, DVD, Internet, Wi-Fi. In-hotel: bar, golf course, tennis courts, pool, gym, spa, beachfront, bicycles, laundry facilities, Wi-Fi, parking (free), some pets allowed, no-smoking rooms* ⊟*AE, D, MC, V* ⦿*EP.*

$$$$ ▧**Regent Palms.** High on luxury and glitz, this is a place to ☾ see and be seen. The infinity pool, one of the chicest in the Caribbean, has sun pods (round, white cushioned loungers), a swim-up bar, and iPods to borrow. Suites, which have colonial-style furnishings and luxurious bedding and appointments, have two or three bedrooms but can be subdivided to create one-bedroom suites and regular rooms (which will have only a kitchenette); all bedrooms have a separate terrace. One big plus for families is a washer and dryer in all but regular rooms. The spa is stunning, offering every treatment imaginable; it certainly ranks among the best in the Caribbean. A new feature in the rooms is access to every radio station in the world, so you can hear reports from back home while you're in paradise. **Pros:** great people-watching; lively atmosphere; one of the best spas in the Caribbean. **Cons:** some would say busy not lively; a little formal and stuffy (cover-ups are required when you go to the pool). ⊠*Grace Bay* ☎*649/946–8666* ⊕*www.regent hotels.com* ⇋*72 suites* ⌂*In-room: safe, kitchen (some), DVD, Wi-Fi. In-hotel: 2 restaurants, room service, bar, tennis court, pool, gym, spa, beachfront, water sports, children's programs (ages 4–12), laundry facilities, Wi-Fi* ⊟*AE, D, MC, V* ⦿*BP.*

$$$–$$$$ ▧**Royal West Indies Resort.** With a contemporary take on colonial architecture and the outdoor feel of a botanical garden, this unpretentious resort has plenty of garden-view and beachfront studios and suites for moderate self-catering budgets. Room 135 on the western corner has the most dramatic ocean views. Right on Grace Bay Beach, the property has a small restaurant and bar for poolside cocktails and dining. Ask at the reception desk for help and advice on where to go explore. Special packages and free-night offers are available during the low season. **Pros:** the best

bang for the buck on Provo; on one of the widest stretches of Grace Bay Beach. **Cons:** Club Med next door can be noisy; construction on the other side. *⌂Box 482, Grace Bay* ☎*649/946–5004 or 800/332–4203* ⊕*www.royal westindies.com* ⌖*99 suites* &*In-room: safe, kitchen, Internet. In-hotel: restaurant, bar, pools, beachfront, water sports, bicycles, laundry facilities, laundry service, no-smoking rooms* ☰*AE, MC, V* ⏷*EP.*

$$$–$$$$ ▧**Sands at Grace Bay.** Spacious gardens and two pools are surrounded by six rather impersonal three-story buildings at this otherwise well-appointed resort. Guests can expect friendly and helpful staff and excellent amenities, including a spa, good-size fitness room, and a beachside cabana restaurant called Hemingway's. Sparkling ocean views from huge screened patios and floor-to-ceiling windows are best in the oceanfront suites in Blocks 3 and 4, which are also closest to the beach, restaurant, and pool. A complete renovation in 2007 added a beautiful new lobby and made the rooms more luxurious. **Pros:** one of the best places for families; central location near shops and numerous restaurants; screened balconies and porches give an escape from incessant air-conditioning. **Cons:** a new wooden pool deck can cause splinters, so keep an eye on the kids; avoid courtyard rooms, which are not worth the price. *⌂Box 681, Grace Bay* ☎*649/941–5199 or 877/777–2637* ⊕*www. thesandsresort.com* ⌖*118 suites* &*In-room: safe, kitchen (some), Internet, Wi-Fi. In-hotel: restaurant, bar, tennis court, pools, gym, spa, beachfront, water sports, bicycles, laundry facilities, laundry service, Internet terminal, no-smoking rooms, some pets allowed* ☰*AE, MC, V* ⏷*EP.*

$–$$ ▧**Sibonné.** Dwarfed by most of the nearby resorts, the smallest hotel on Grace Bay Beach has snug (by Provo's spacious standards) but pleasant rooms with Bermuda-style balconies and a completely circular but tiny pool. The pool is hardly used because the property is right on the beach. Rooms on the second floor have airy, vaulted ceilings; downstairs rooms have views of and access to the attractively planted courtyard garden, replete with palms, yellow elder, and exotic birdlife. The popular beachfront Bay Bistro serves breakfast, lunch, and dinner. Book early to get one of the two simple, value rooms or the beachfront apartment, complete with four-poster bed, which is four steps from the beach; all three are usually reserved months in advance. **Pros:** closest property to the beach; the island's best bargain directly on the beach. **Cons:** pool is small and dated. ✉*Princess Dr., Box 144, Grace Bay* ☎*649/946–5547 or 800/528–1905* ⊕*www.sibonne.com* ⤶*29 rooms, 1 apartment* ⚲*In-room: safe. In-hotel: restaurant, bar, pool, beachfront, water sports, bicycles, laundry service* ⊟*AE, MC, V* ⦿❘*CP.*

★ **Fodors**Choice ⚏ **The Somerset.** This luxury resort has the "wow"
$$$$ factor, starting with the architecture, followed by the service, and ending in your luxuriously appointed suite. What sets the Somerset apart is that it's more focused on your comfort and enjoyment than in attracting a celebrity clientele. A laid-back unpretentiousness means you don't have to dress up to go to the pool. Unmatched service makes you feel at home. A modern pool deck is equipped with a resistance pool and underwater speakers. The oversized suites are equipped with such extras as a plasma TV, an Xbox system, a wine chiller, and Viking appliances, including a washer and dryer, so you don't need to pack heavily. The English Cottages are multistory town homes with 15-foot ceilings in the living rooms; the Stirling House residences all have ocean and pool views; the Estate Villas, which take up an entire floor, are the most stunning, with cathedral ceilings and private hot tubs outside on the balconies. The red tile roofs and oversized balconies compliment the turquoise ocean beautifully; the beachfront is on one of the best sections of Grace Bay. It doesn't get better than this. **Pros:** the most beautiful architecture on Provo; terrific service; Wednesday movie nights out on the lawn. **Cons:** having to leave; the cheapest lock-out rooms are not worth the cost. ✉*Princess Dr., Grace Bay* ☎*649/946–5900* ⊕*www.thesomerset.com* ⤶*53 suites* ⚲*In-room: safe, kitchen, DVD, Wi-Fi. In-hotel: restaurant, room service, bar, pool, gym, beachfront, water sports, bicycles, children's programs (ages 3–16), Wi-Fi, laundry facilities* ⊟*AE, MC, V* ⦿❘*CP.*

$$$ ⚏**Tradewinds Condotel.** Often overlooked by vacationers, Tradewinds gives a fair amount for your money. It sits behind Point Grace and in front of Saltmills Plaza, a central location. All the units are one-bedroom suites with separate bedrooms and full kitchens. The furniture is dark wood with Italian touches, with pale-yellow walls and linens. While Tradewinds may not have all the bells and whistles of a resort, it's a great self-catering place that's clean, comfortable, and a good value. The balconies look out onto the nicely landscaped pool, and some even have views of Grace Bay. Across the street is Saltmills Plaza and Regent

Village—you're within walking distance of most of the shops and restaurants on Grace Bay Road. You'll have access to all of the restaurants on the beach, too. **Pros:** even though it's not on the beach, some rooms still have views; central location within walking distance of everything you need; washer and dryer in every unit. **Cons:** not on the beach; self-catering with no resort facilities or services. ⊠*Grace Bay Rd., Grace Bay* ☎*649/946–5194* ⊕*www. Tradewindscondotel.com* ⟿*48 suites* ⌂*In-room: safe, kitchen, DVD (some), Wi-Fi. In-hotel: pool, bicycles, laundry facilities, parking (free), no-smoking rooms* ⊟*AE, D, MC, V* |○|*EP.*

$$$$ ⊞**Turks & Caicos Club.** On the quieter, western end of Grace
★ Bay, this intimate all-suites hotel is one of a handful with a gated entrance. The buildings are colonial-style with lovely gingerbread trim. Though the resort aims for an aura of exclusivity, the staff is warm and friendly. Safari-themed suites, complete with raised four-poster beds and spacious balconies, are a definite plus at this quiet retreat. This gorgeous boutique hotel is a true hotel, one of only a few on Provo that doesn't sell rooms to vacationers; since the hotel doesn't have to accommodate condo owners, you are more likely to get a room request honored. The rates include a full American breakfast. Check the Web site for unique packages, including one with a professional photographer. **Pros:** incredible, lush grounds; on one of the best stretches of Grace Bay Beach; great snorkeling from the beach. **Cons:** small bathrooms. ⊠*West Grace Bay Beach, Box 687, West Grace Bay* ☎*649/946–5800 or 888/482–2582* ⊕*www.turksandcaicosclub.com* ⟿*21 suites* ⌂*In-room: safe, DVD, Wi-Fi, kitchen. In-hotel: restaurant, room service, bar, pool, gym, beachfront, water sports, bicycles, laundry facilities, Wi-Fi* ⊟*AE, MC, V* ☺*Closed Sept.* |○|*BP.*

$$$$ ⊞**The Tuscany.** This luxury, gated condo complex at the end of Grace Bay Beach is gorgeous. All the condos have three bedrooms with designer furnishings and spacious balconies with oceanfront views; each condo also has three baths and a laundry room, which makes sharing a breeze even if you're not family. Lined by palm trees, the pool has a Tuscan feel and is one of the most beautiful on Provo. Guests receive a cell phone, which comes preset with numbers for island restaurants and excursion companies, for use wherever they go during their stay. **Pros:** luxurious; all condos have ocean views; beautiful pool. **Cons:** no restaurant and far from the best restaurants; very expensive for self-catering. ☏*Box 623, Grace Bay* ☎*649/941–4667* ⊕*www.the tuscanyresort.com* ⇨*30 condos* ⚐*In-room: kitchen. In-hotel: tennis court, pool, gym, beachfront, Wi-Fi* ⊟*AE, MC, V* ☉*EP.*

$$$$ ☒**Villa Del Mar.** This resort, which just opened in 2008, offers some tremendous features for the price, even though it is not directly on Grace Bay Beach. Managed by the same company that runs West Bay Club, Ambergris Cay, and the Greenbrier Resort in West Virginia, Villa Del Mar is ideal for the vacationer who loves to eat outside the resort, as it is located within walking distance of some of Provo's best restaurants. It's less than a minute's walk from the beach. There are nice touches like granite countertops and plasma TVs. Breakfast is included. **Pros:** close to the best restaurants on the island; within walking distance of Casablanca Casino; continental breakfast included in rate. **Cons:** no on-site restaurant; no views from most floors; not directly on the beach. ✉*Cresent Rd., Grace Bay* ☎*649/941–5160* ⊕*www.YourVillaDelMar.com* ⇨*18 rooms, 24 suites* ⚐*In-room: safe, kitchen, DVD, Wi-Fi. In-hotel: bar, pools, gym, laundry facilities, laundry service, Wi-Fi, parking (free), no-smoking rooms* ⊟*AE, D, MC, V* ☉*CP.*

$$$$ ☒**Villa Renaissance.** This is luxury for the self-catering tourist. Although it's not a full-service resort, guests do get daily maid service, afternoon tea or coffee at the Pavillion Bar, and a weekly manager's cocktail reception. There is no restaurant on-site, but the location puts you within walking distance of some of the island's best restaurants. The front desk is always willing to help with concierge service. There is a lighted tennis court, a fitness center, and bicycles. The gorgeous suites have stunning balconies or patios facing the ocean. Resembling a small Tuscan village square, it is one of the most beautiful buildings on Provo. **Pros:** luxury for less; one of the prettiest courtyards in Provo. **Cons:** no restaurant; not full-service resort. ☏*Box 592, Grace Bay* ☎*649/941–5300 or 877/285–8764* ⊕*www. villarenaissance.com* ⇨*20 suites* ⚐*In-room: safe, kitchen, DVD. In-hotel: bar, pool, spa, beachfront, bicycles, laundry facilities* ⊟*AE, MC, V* ☉*EP.*

★ **Fodors**Choice ☒**West Bay Club.** One of Provo's newest resorts
$$$$ has a prime location on a pristine stretch of Grace Bay Beach and encourages repeat visits. It offers a quiet elegance with a contemporary, slightly Asian feel. All rooms

are appointed with dark-wood furniture and cabinetry complimented with lighter bath and kitchen fixtures that give a contemporary feel. The rooms have all the latest design touches, including plasma TVs, plush couches, and beautiful marble tiles in earth tones and turquoise. You will need to decide whether to relax on a quiet and soothing section of beach or lie next to the lusciously landscaped pool. The location is ideal, away from the main hub so relaxing is optimized, yet steps away from the best off-the-beach snorkeling. **Pros:** all rooms have a beach view; new, clean, and sparkling; contemporary architecture makes it stand out from other resorts. **Cons:** a car is needed to go shopping and to the best restaurants. ⊠*Lower Bight Rd., Lower Bight* ☎*649/946–8550* ⊕*www.TheWestBayClub. com* ⟑*46 suites* ⟐*In-room: safe, kitchen, DVD, Internet, Wi-Fi. In-hotel: restaurant, room service, bar, pool, gym, spa, beachfront, water sports, laundry facilities, laundry service, Wi-Fi, parking (free), no-smoking rooms* ⊟*AE, D, MC, V* ⏀*EP.*

★ Fodor'sChoice ⊡ **Windsong Resort.** On a gorgeous beach lined
$$$ with several appealing resorts, Windsong stands out for two reasons: an active Snuba program and a magnificent pool. Snuba allows uncertified divers to get closer to the reef than snorkelers can, while the air tank is left on the surface. The resort's pool is an original—rails made of glass don't obstruct views, and there's a sunken restaurant and a bridge overhead. The sunken restaurant, though outdoors, has air-conditioning and a glass wall that allows parents to eat while they watch children swim. The architecture is pure Caribbean, with yellow walls and white balconies contrasting with the turquoise sea. The interiors include beautiful marble floors, oversized bathrooms, and stainless-steel appliances. Ask for a corner unit, where the walls of windows in the living room open up to give a feeling of being outdoors. The penthouse suites have rooftop patios with lounge chairs and endless private views of Grace Bay Beach; soon it will have hot tubs and wet bars. Note: the restaurant was not open at this writing but was scheduled to open in early 2009. **Pros:** the pool is the coolest; great Snuba program; gorgeous new resort. **Cons:** resort is experiencing some growing pains, so service can be lacking; studios have only a refrigerator and microwave; thinner stretch of beachfront here. ⊠*Stubbs Rd., Lower Bight* ☎*649/941–7700* ⊕*www.WindsongResort.com* ⟑*16 studios, 30 suites* ⟐*In-room: safe, kitchen (some), refrigerator,*

DVD. In-hotel: restaurant, room service, bars, pool, gym, beachfront, water sports, children's programs (ages 3 to 16), laundry facilities, Internet terminal, Wi-Fi, parking (free), no-smoking rooms ☰AE, MC, V ⓘEP.

TURTLE COVE

$–$$ ☒**Turtle Cove Inn.** This pleasant two-story inn offers affordable and comfortable lodging in Turtle Cove Marina. All rooms have either a private balcony or patio overlooking the lush tropical gardens and pool or the marina. Besides the dockside Aqua Bar and Terrace, there's also a souvenir shop and liquor store. The inn is ideally situated for divers looking to roll from their beds into the ocean. **Pros:** very reasonable prices for Provo; nice marina views; popular and inexpensive restaurant. **Cons:** not on the beach; requires a car to get around. *⊠Turtle Cove Marina, Box 131, Turtle Cove ☎649/946–4203 or 800/887–0477 ⊕www.turtle coveinn.com ⇨28 rooms, 2 suites ⚿In-room: safe, Internet, refrigerator. In-hotel: restaurant, bar, pool, bicycles, no-smoking rooms ☰AE, D, MC, V ⓘEP.*

ELSEWHERE ON PROVIDENCIALES

$$$$ ☒**Amanyara.** If you seek seclusion, peace, and tranquillity in a Zen-like atmosphere, this is your place. All accommodations are in pavilions, which are simply furnished with an Asian minimalist flair yet have such luxuries as TVs, DVD players, and surround-sound systems. A movie room and well-stocked library are among the few entertainment options, but small touches, such as a shoe rack at the beach and huggers to keep your bottled water cool, are welcome. No need to sign for anything here—the staff will always remember you by name. When it comes to dining, expect an Asian-influenced menu and very high prices. One thing is for certain; it's a long, pricey ride to other restaurants, not to mention other excursions. This is a place to come if you are looking for peace and quiet in a remote location on a stunning beach. There is construction on-site, but you can't see it from the beach. A unique feature is that rates include the minibar (except spirits) and all long-distance phone calls. **Pros:** on one of the best beaches on Provo; resort is quiet and secluded. **Cons:** isolated; far from restaurants, excursions, and other beaches. *⊠Northwest Point ☎649/941–8133 ⊕www.amanresorts.com ⇨40 pavilions ⚿In-room: safe, refrigerator, DVD. In-hotel: 2 restaurants, room service, bar, tennis courts, pool, gym, spa, beachfront, diving, water sports ☰AE, MC, V ⓘEP.*

$$$$ ⊠**Nikki Beach Resort Turks & Caicos Islands.** You may think that someone transported this très-chic resort from Miami's South Beach to Provo. Everything is white-on-white, with gauze curtains on day beds and benches scattered in the sand. If you like an active social scene and people-watching, look no further. The parties here are about as wild as things get in Provo, with girls dancing on the pool bar. The rooms are modern and hip, with all the luxuries you would expect at this upscale price. (Check out the unusual treats in the minibar—you won't find these elsewhere on Provo.) Music mixes made exclusively for Nikki Beach Resorts is piped all day outdoors, adding to the party ambience. Once a month the famous White Party attracts some of the world's most popular jet-setters. While the resort does allow children to stay in rooms, kids under 12 are not allowed at the restaurant and pool on weekends when adult activities are going on, including the Sunday champagne parties. **Pros:** chic nightlife; close to the marina; Sunday brunch and monthly White Parties are entertaining. **Cons:** late-night music might keep you from sleeping; it's not on Grace Bay. ⊠ *Leeward Marina, Leeward Going Through* ☎*649/941–3747* ⊕*www.NikkiBeachHotels.com* ⥽*16 rooms, 32 suites* ⚭*In-room: safe, refrigerator, DVD, Wi-Fi. In-hotel: restaurant, room service, bars, gym, beachfront, laundry facilities, laundry service, Internet terminal, Wi-Fi, parking (free), no-smoking rooms* ⊟*AE, MC, V* ⏐⊚*EP.*

$$$$ ⊠**Northwest Point Resort.** Miles from anywhere and completely on its own, this resort should be your destination if you need complete solitude. In fact, the resort is so isolated that the paved road ends even before you reach the front gates and continues as packed sand. The Spanish-style resort itself is quite nice, with white walls and arches, red-tile roofs, and gorgeous landscaping; it's impeccably clean. Rooms are spacious, with full kitchens and large balconies that face the ocean. The colors are tropical, the wood furniture is light, and the rooms have everything you need for comfort. The quiet pool area is colorfully framed by flowers, and there's even a hot tub. A path leads through a huge gazebo and beyond to the beach. The beach here has a lot of sea grass, but the resort rakes it daily. While this is no Grace Bay, it's a long, uninterrupted stretch of sand, great for solitary walks. This is also the best area in Provo for scuba diving—Northwest Point is where all of the companies bring divers. You need a car if you stay here; the restaurant is open only from November to August and serves only breakfast and lunch. **Pros:** landscaping is lush and well maintained; kitchens allow you to do some cooking on your own. **Cons:** on a grassy beach that's more attractive to turtles than swimmers; far from everything; restaurant only opens seasonally and has limited service. ⊠*Northwest Point* ☏*649/941–8961* ⊕*www.Northwest PointResort.com* ⌂*49 rooms* △*In-room: safe, kitchen, DVD, Wi-Fi. In-hotel: restaurant, bar, pool, gym, beachfront, water sports, laundry facilities, Wi-Fi, parking (free), some pets allowed, no-smoking rooms* ⌕*3-night minimum during peak season* ⊟*AE, D, MC, V* ⦿*EP.*

PRIVATE VILLAS

On Provo you can rent a self-catering villa or private home. For the best villa selection, make your reservations three to six months in advance, or you may not get your first choice. Most villas can be rented on multiple villa-rental sites, depending on the management company.

RENTAL AGENTS

Prestigious Properties (⌖*Prestige Pl., Grace Bay* ☏*649/946–5355* ⊕*www.prestigiousproperties.com*) offers a wide selection of modest to magnificent villas in the Leeward, Grace Bay, and Turtle Cove areas of Providenciales.

T. C. Safari (☏*649/941–5043* ⊕*www.tcsafari.tc*) has exclusive oceanfront properties in the beautiful and tranquil Sapodilla Bay–Chalk Sound neighborhood on Provo's southwest shores.

TC Villas (⌖*2970 Peachtree Rd., Atlanta, GA* ☏*404/467–4858* ⊕*www.TCVillas.com*) has hand-selected the most beautiful villas in Provo and has a wide selection from one-bedroom cottages to private estates.

RECOMMENDED PRIVATE VILLAS

$$$ ⌂**Acacia Villa.** On a canal in the prestigious Leeward Going Through neighborhood, you'll feel like you have found a home away from home. The villa comes complete with a full kitchen, 42-inch plasma TV, DVD player, and blenders to make tropical drinks. The dark-wood furniture contrasts with bright linens to give an Old Caribbean feel. The cathedral ceilings create an open feeling, and the living room looks down on the private pool, where there is a separate bathroom. There's also a private dock. The owners live next door, so you will be well taken care of. There are kayaks to use on the canal, and Nikki Beach Club is just

a short walk away for entertainment. Another short walk leads you to Leeward Beach, where you'll find beach umbrellas and solitude. Grace Bay, with its glorious beach, shops, and excellent restaurants, is only minutes away. **Pros:** owners live on-island, ensuring a nice stay; pretty pool area and patio; there's an alarm (though no on-site security); airport pick-up included. **Cons:** need a car to get around; not on the beach; air-conditioning is only in bedrooms and for an additional charge. ⊠*Pinta Lane, Leeward Going Through* ☎*649/941–8736* ⊕*www.AcaciaVilla.com* ⇘*2 bedrooms, 2½ baths* ⟁*No a/c (some), dishwasher,DVD, Wi-Fi, pool, laundry facilities, no kids under 12, no smoking* ⊟*No credit cards* ⟐*EP* ☞*1-week min.*

$$$ ⊞**Aquamarine Beach Houses.** This cluster of three houses sits on Grace Bay Beach and has the best location of any villa in the area; though close to the main hub, you won't find a more secluded beachfront than this. The only villas directly on Grace Bay Beach, they include various combinations of one to 17 bedrooms (you can rent individual sections with one to four bedrooms), with a huge shared pool, tennis court, and beach volleyball court. Refurbished in 2008, they have beautiful tile floors and completely new kitchens. The owner, Paula, can make recommendations for you, show you how to get around, and even set up a wedding for you. The use of kayaks, snorkel equipment, and boogie boards is included. **Pros:** you can't stay closer to the beach anywhere else; owner lives on property; air-conditioning (bedrooms only) is included in the rates. **Cons:** car required to get to the restaurants and shops. ⊠*Grace Bay Rd., Lower Bight* ☎*649/941–5690* ⊕*www.AquamarineBeachHouses.com* ⇘*5 bedrooms, 3 baths (Sunrise Villa); 8 bedrooms, 4 baths (Sanddune Villa); 3 bedrooms, 2 baths (Sunrise Beach House)* ⟁*No a/c (some), safe, dishwasher (some), DVD, Internet, Wi-Fi, daily maid service, fully staffed, tennis court, pool, beachfront, water toys, laundry facilities* ⊟*AE, D, DC, MC, V* ⟐*EP* ☞*4-night min.*

$$$$ ⊞**Bajacu.** The coral walls of this majestic villa, which sits high up on the hill at Turtle Tail and has been featured in countless magazines, can be spotted from miles away. With its hand-painted walls and tiles to the custom-designed, poured-concrete bed and couch platforms (which are covered with thick multicolored pillows and cushions), this has to be the most exotic villa on Provo. Porches and hallways connect all rooms, affording privacy but connecting to common areas. The best feature is the stunning infinity pool that wraps around the house, allowing each guest to step out of a bedroom directly into the water. The views are endless; different shades of turquoise of the Caicos Banks can be seen from every room. Most furnishings are made from antique teak from Bali; the walls are hand-painted to look like tile. An on-call staff lives behind the villa, so you need never see the kitchen, even in the middle of the night. While the cook will prepare all your meals, you must pay for food separately. **Pros:** private and secluded; fully staffed to meet your every need; pool seems to float off the hill. **Cons:** need a high-clearance vehicle to get up the rough road to the villa; not on a particularly good stretch of beach; extremely expensive. ⊠*Ocean Dr., Turtle Tail* ⊕*www.Bajacu.com* ⬲*5 bedrooms, 5 bathrooms* ☝ *Safe, dishwasher, DVD, Wi-Fi, daily maid service, on-site security, fully staffed, pools, gym, laundry facilities, no-smoking rooms* ⊟*AE, MC, V* ⏿*EP* ⚷*1-week min.*

$$$$ ⊞**Ballyhoo Cottage/Callaloo Cottage.** Side-by-side twin cottages are beachfront at the entrance to Turtle Cove Marina. Each is constructed from hand-carved bricks, and each private pool is created from million-year-old nonslip coral stone and has a picturesque gazebo. Ideal for couples, each villa allows a maximum of two people—and no kids. Tall cathedral ceilings add space, and the rooms have beautiful French doors opening up to the pool and the beach beyond. Ballyhoo is decorated in colorful tropical prints and is rented from Saturday to Saturday; Callaloo is decorated in ocean colors, earth tones, and soft turquoises, and is rented from Sunday to Sunday. The cottages are a five-minute walk from the excellent restaurants at Turtle Cove and from excursions at the marina. **Pros:** perfect space for one couple; romantic and secluded; both beachfront and private pool. **Cons:** no children allowed; alarm but no on-site security. ⊠*Coconut Rd., Turtle Cove* ⊕*www.TCVillas.com* ⬲*2 cottages, each with 1 bedroom, 1 bath* ☝*Safe, dishwasher, DVD, Wi-Fi, weekly maid service, pool, beachfront, laundry facilities, some pets allowed, no kids, no smoking* ⊟ *No credit cards* ⏿*EP* ⚷*1-week min.*

★ **Fodor's**Choice ⊞**Coriander Cottage.** The perfect villa for a
$$$$ romantic getaway or small family is close to the beach at Turtle Cove and has unobstructed views from an elevated gazebo next to the pool, so you can sip coffee while you gaze at the ocean. Smith Cove beach, reachable by a path through the "backyard," has excellent snorkeling. The interior has a nautical theme; the stone walls are decorated

with ship masts, boats, and tin fish. The small kitchen is compact yet has everything you'll need, including stainless-steel appliances and granite countertops. It's an easy walk to Turtle Cove Marina, which has numerous restaurants, shops, and entertainment, including the Players Club Casino and Sharkbites for Friday happy hours, but it's far enough away from the bustle that you won't hear any noise at night. Though fully air-conditioned, the air-conditioning is metered and charged after a $100 allowance. **Pros:** perfect for a romantic getaway; in front of excellent snorkeling reef; walking distance to restaurants. **Cons:** no children allowed; can only rent Saturday to Saturday. ⊠*North Shore, Turtle Cove* ⊕*www.TcVillas.com* ⬞*1 bedroom, 1 bathroom* ⬞*Dishwasher, DVD, Wi-Fi, weekly maid service, on-site security, pool, beachfront, water toys, laundry facilities, no smoking* ⊟*No credit cards* ⊙*EP* ⬞*1-week min.*

★ Fodor's Choice ⬞**Crystal Sands Villa on the Beach.** This beautiful
$$$ two-story villa on Sapodilla Bay has two bedrooms on each
☾ floor, and you can rent one floor or the whole house. Expect all the comforts of home but in a more beautiful location. On each floor a huge kitchen opens up to the living room, great for entertaining. The oversized patio and balcony are great places to try to see the "green flash." Bamboo and wicker furniture remind you that you are in the tropics. The bedrooms are identical, and each has a private bath and walk-in closet. The owners live on-island, and will recommend excursions and restaurants. Sapodilla Bay is knee-deep for hundreds of yards, making it perfect for children, yet it's also tranquil, ideal for a romantic retreat. Maid service is available for a midweek clean-up for an additional charge. **Pros:** directly on a beautiful beach; a beautiful home for the money; owners on-island. **Cons:** you need a car to get around; central air-conditioning is throughout but is metered and charged separately. ⊠*Chalk Sound Rd., Sapodilla Bay* ☎*649/941–7440* ⊕*www.crystal sandsvilla.com* ⬞*4 bedrooms, 4 baths* ⬞ *Dishwasher, DVD, Wi-Fi, pool, beachfront, water toys, no smoking* ⊟*MC, V* ⊙*EP* ⬞*1-week min.*

$$ ⬞**Harbour Club Villas.** Off the beaten path, these moderately priced villas are rustic, comfortable, and charming without giving up such amenities as satellite TV, a full kitchen, and air-conditioning in the bedrooms. Though not close to the beach, you're close to the marina used by all the dive shops and tour operators, making these small homes ideal if you're looking for water excursions at a great price. The

six villas front Flamingo Pond, an excellent place to practice bonefishing and visit the resident flamingos. The owners, Barry and Marta, live on the property and ensure your stay is comfortable; they will tidy up while you explore and make recommendations. After your diving adventures, gather around the shared pool and tell tales with the other guests. You might come as a tourist, but you'll leave as a friend. **Pros:** terrific bargain for the active diving crowd. **Cons:** not close to beaches; need a car to get around. ✉ *Venetian Rd., Turtle Tail* ☎*649/941–5748* ⊕*www.HarbourClubVillas.com* ⇆*6 villas with 1 bedroom, 1 bath* ♢ *No a/c (some), no phone, safe, Wi-Fi, daily maid service, pool, water toys, no smoking* ☐*AE, MC, V* ℺ *EP* ⌁*3-night min.*

★ **Fodors Choice** ⌂ **Pelican Nest.** These side-by-side, brand-new
$$$$ villas are some of the best-kept secrets in Provo. In the Leeward area of Grace Bay, the property has a private pathway that leads to a secluded section of Leeward Beach, offering access all the way down to Grace Bay Beach. Choose between two villas (Cocoa Villa is larger), each with a private pool and huge patio for outdoor dining. In each a state-of-the-art kitchen opens to a living room with cathedral ceiling; sliding-glass doors open to the private pool and bring in ocean breezes. Four-poster beds have tropical linens and palm fans for a true Caribbean feel. Gas grills help you maximize your outdoor time. The property owners own the land fronting the beach, so there will always be a view. You can walk all the way down Grace Bay Beach if you want a more lively atmosphere, yet retreat to your personal stretch of paradise whenever it gets to be too much. **Pros:** impeccably furnished; on a private, gorgeous stretch of beach; owner on-island. **Cons:** this is a residential neighborhood, so a car is a necessity; central air (throughout) is metered and charged separately. ✉*Sunset Dr., Leeward Going Through* ⊕*www.pelicannest.tc* ⇆*2 villas, each with 3 bedrooms, 3½ baths* ♢ *DVD, Wi-Fi, pool, laundry facilities, no smoking* ☐*AE, MC, V* ℺*EP* ⌁*1-week min.*

$$$$ ⌂ **Three Cays Villa.** With tropical-yellow walls and red-tile roof, this Mediterranean-style villa stands out from others on Provo. Inside the colorful walls of coral and blue, the home is bright and cheery. A two-story library has floor-to-ceiling bookshelves and a ladder and is fully stocked. A guesthouse adds an additional bedroom—its bathroom is open to the outside and has an outdoor shower. The villa is air-conditioned throughout. The landscaping is impeccable, with levels of lush plants and steps down to a pool that would make a great setting for a small, romantic wedding. Although the villa is on the water, it's not directly on the beach; there are steps through the coral to the water for swimming. The children's play area is a nice plus. The location affords great privacy; however, a high-clearance vehicle would make the ride on the rough road to the villa more comfortable. **Pros:** an outside courtyard that would make a gorgeous backdrop for a wedding; colorful walls liven the mood; oceanfront but not beachfront. **Cons:** car needed; a rough road leads to the villa, making a high-clearance vehicle preferable; alarm system and electronic gate but no on-site security. ⊠*Bristol Hill Dr., Juba Salina* ⊕*www.ThreeCaysVilla.com* ⇨ *4 bedrooms, 5 baths* ⟁*Dishwasher, DVD, TV, pool, laundry facilities, no smoking* ⊟*AE, MC, V* ⫿⊙⫿*EP* ⟋*1-week min.*

$$$$ ⊞**Vieux Caribe.** At this location between Sapodilla Bay and Taylor Bay you'll be hard-pressed to decide which nearby secluded beach to visit. The villa itself—one of the original vacation homes on Provo, with an old-world, plantation feel—is huge, with three stories, cathedral ceilings, and spacious rooms; each bedroom has its own private balcony. There are two hammocks on the top floor, with its commanding views of gorgeous Taylor Bay. The oversized sofas and armoires are Balinese-style, made from carved, distressed teak. Although there is an extra charge for air-conditioning after an initial $150 allowance, there are six separate zones in the house, so you can cool individual rooms. The pool area has a grill, and the house comes with all the beach toys you need, including snorkel equipment, buckets, pails, floats, and noodles. The private dock is a rarity, and the views of turquoise Taylor Bay are mindblowing. You can't help but relax here, with its private location and quiet surroundings. **Pros:** gorgeous views from every room; every bedroom has a private balcony. **Cons:** can only rent Saturday to Saturday; alarm but no on-site security; car necessary; oceanfront but not directly on a beach. ⊠*Ocean Point Dr., Taylor Bay* ⊕*www.TcVillas.com* ⇨*5 bedrooms, 5 baths* ⟁*Safe, dishwasher, DVD, Wi-Fi, weekly maid service, pool, tennis court, water toys, laundry facilities, no smoking* ⊟*No credit cards* ⫿⊙⫿*EP* ⟋*1-week min.*

$$$$ ⊞**Villa Avalon.** In Turtle Cove, Villa Avalon offers a little bit of everything. It's quiet and secluded yet within walking

distance of numerous restaurants, shops, and a small casino. It has its own isolated beach. The rocky beachfront has the best off-the-beach snorkeling on the island, yet you can walk a short distance to a sandy area for swimming. The architecture is pure California, with arches, stucco, and tiled roofs. The property consists of a series of free-standing structures connected by porches and outdoor hallways, so each room affords complete privacy and has its own entrance; but guests can meet in the communal pool, kitchen, and living room. The comfortable great room offers stunning views and has a large-screen TV. All bedrooms have pool views and their own luxury bathroom; however, except for the master suite (which has a claw-foot tub and an outdoor shower in its gigantic bath), the remaining rooms have low ceilings and are small. The dining room is outdoors under arches and a soaring ceiling. Rentals are only from Saturday to Saturday. **Pros:** outdoor entertaining area with swim-up bar is out of this world; great snorkeling off the beach; walking distance to numerous restaurants. **Cons:** the smaller bedrooms seem dark and boxy compared to the rest of the house; air-conditioning (throughout) is metered and charged after an initial $150 allotment; alarm but no on-site security. ⊠*Coconut Rd., Turtle Cove* ⊕*www. tcvillas.com* ⊸*4 bedrooms, 4 bathrooms* ⌂ *Safe, dishwasher, DVD, Wi-Fi, weekly maid service, pool, beachfront, water toys, laundry facilities, no smoking* ⊟*No credit cards* ⏏*EP* ⌖*1-week min.*

$$$$ 🏠**Villa Balinese.** Villa Balinese, in the Turtle Tail area of Provo on top of coral cliffs facing the bright turquoise shallows of the Caicos Banks, may take your breath away. You'll find 30-foot ceilings with floor-to-ceiling windows that open up to the infinity pool and to the Caicos Banks beyond. The inside walls are hand-cut coral-stone bricks. The furnishings are traditional Balinese, including four-poster beds with flowing curtains and made from carved, distressed woods, in a very modern, Asian-accented setting. The coconut-wood-lined closets add to the exotic feel. TVs are hidden in coffee tables and raised or lowered by remote control. A path through the coral cliffs leads to a bamboo pavilion with a daybed and then to a small waterside dock. The private deck offers the ideal spot from which to view the island's famed glowworms, which come out four or five days after a full moon. **Pros:** beautiful home; private and secluded. **Cons:** not close to a beach; need a car to get around; cost of air-conditioning not included. ⊠*Ocean*

Renting Directly from the Owner

CLOSE UP

Not all resort rooms and villas need to be rented from management companies. By renting directly from the owner you can get the same room or home you would rent through a management company for less. Expect savings of up to 25% off company rates. You'll also save a 5% service charge. You may not get daily maid service, but everything else the resort or villa has to offer will be included. Check out ⊕ *www.homeaway.com* or the very excellent ⊕ *www.vrbo.com* for listings.

2

Dr., Turtle Tail ☎*649/341–2338* ⊕*www.prestigiousproperties.com* ▭*3 bedrooms, 3 baths* ⌂*Dishwasher, DVD, Wi-Fi, weekly maid service, fully staffed, hot tub, pool, laundry facilities, no children under 12, no smoking* ▭*AE, MC, V* ⊚*EP* ⌁*1-week min.*

$$$$ ⊡**Villa Palmera.** If you require seclusion, look no further than this villa perched 40 feet above the sea and with endless views of the ocean from every room. The location, far off the beaten path in Thompson Cove, means you'll have the ocean all to yourself. The villa is loaded with luxuries. The gorgeous kitchen has a large island with lots of seating; professional-grade appliances, including a built-in refrigerator; and stunning ocean views. The living room is open and spacious, with 35-foot ceilings, a 50-inch plasma TV, and an iPod docking station. There's a small gym with Bowflex and elliptical machines, a treadmill, and free weights, all with a water view. The villa consists of several different levels of decks, balconies, and gazebos; one gazebo contains the dining area, one has a built-in couch covered with thick cushions. The infinity pool is on a patio under two stories of arches flanked by the two gazebos. The bottom floor has indoor and outdoor showers. There is a small deck for snorkeling and a small beach for tanning, though the decks could use a little TLC. The inside, however, is immaculate and comfortable. Another suite with a separate entrance can be rented for $1,500. A representative from the management company will greet you at the airport and lead you to the villa. **Pros:** not a home but a mansion; private and secluded. **Cons:** off the beaten path, so a car is

necessary; air-conditioning (throughout) charged after a $150 allotment; although there is a beach, it's tiny and more rocks than sand. ✉Thompson Cove ⊕www.TcVillas. com ⇨6 bedrooms, 7 bathrooms ☖Safe, DVD, Wi-Fi, pool, gym, beachfront, laundry facilities, no smoking ⊟No credit cards ⏁EP ⏁1-week min.

$$$$ ☷**Villa Paprika.** With three stories of arches facing the ocean, this villa, on the north shore near Turtle Cove, offers the island's best snorkeling. Each bedroom has its own bath and private balcony overlooking the pool and ocean. Floor-to-ceiling arched windows add a tropical ambience; high ceilings and an open floor plan add to the spaciousness. The decor includes carved-wood armoires and colorful linens; travertine tiles and marble bathrooms add luxury. The house is divided into zones but fully air-conditioned. There is a kiddie pool and grill under a gazebo, all under those stunning arches—you may never want to come back inside. **Pros:** huge home is big enough for the entire family; great off-the-beach snorkeling. **Cons:** rocky beachfront; alarm system but no on-site security; it's a dark walk at night to nearby restaurants. ✉Coconut Rd., Turtle Cove ⊕www.TCVillas.com ⇨5 bedrooms, 5½ baths ☖Dishwasher, DVD, Wi-Fi, pool, beachfront, laundry facilities, some pets allowed, no smoking ⊟No credit cards ⏁EP ⏁1-week min.

$$$$ ☷**Villa Sandstone.** This villa, one of the originals at North Shore in Turtle Cove, has been impeccably maintained. The two stories are separate but connected by outdoor decks. Two bedrooms are upstairs with the kitchen, living areas, and substantial patio and wraparound porches; three additional bedrooms downstairs have separate outdoor entrances. The decor is casual and comfortable; the huge kitchen is a cook's delight, with all the appliances and utensils you would need. The deck has great views of the sparkling ocean from almost every corner; the hammocks on the deck are made for lazy days. The pool and patio with a grill and lounge chairs afford views of the reef. Directly behind the villa is the best section of Smith's Reef, with colorful fish and a resident stingray. Within walking distance are numerous restaurants, bars, small shops, and the Players Club Casino. **Pros:** walking distance to numerous restaurants; great snorkeling directly from beachfront. **Cons:** some bedrooms only connect to the outside—no fun if it rains; air-conditioning is metered after an initial $150 allotment; alarm but no on-site security ✉Coconut Rd.,

Turtle Cove ⊕*www.TCVillas.com* ➵*5 bedrooms, 5 baths* ⌂*Safe, dishwasher, DVD, Wi-Fi, weekly maid service, pool, beachfront, laundry facilities, some pets allowed, no smoking* ▤*No credit cards* ⎮◯⎮*EP* ⌛*1-week min.*

$$$$ 🏠**Villa Shambala.** A location on Long Bay Beach ensures privacy; in fact, you may find that you often have the beach all to yourself. The rooms are set up in clusters connected by porches and arches, which allows individual privacy yet access to the central public areas. The Bermudian architecture is stunning, with views of the sparkling ocean from every room. Exquisite distressed carved woods and palm-leaf fans create a distinct Caribbean feel. The residence wraps around the infinity pool; a trellis and iron accents give the appearance of a courtyard. The sound system is wired in every room as well as outside, enabling you to play music anywhere you want from your iPod. The latest appliances, including an outdoor built-in gas grill, makes you want to entertain to show off this beautiful house. **Pros:** amazing first impression; Bermudian architecture is gorgeous; on the beach; a cell phone is provided. **Cons:** Long Bay may seem isolated; car required; alarm and gated but no on-site security. ⊠ *Long Bay Beach Rd., Long Bay Hills* ⊕*www.TcVillas.com* ➵*5 bedrooms, 6½ baths* ⌂*Dishwasher, DVD, Wi-Fi, weekly maid service, pool, beachfront, laundry facilities, no smoking* ▤*No credit cards* ⎮◯⎮*EP* ⌛*1-week min.*

$$$$ 🏠**Villa Stonecrest.** One of the more beautiful homes on the island, this is a favorite of families, and it comes with a private dock. The home is fully loaded, and includes TVs in each bedroom, a beautiful pool with floats and beach toys, and two washers and dryers. The bedroom headboards are antique, carved, Balinese doors. Each bedroom has a private terrace facing the ocean. A unique kitchen with blue cabinets adds island flair. Taylor Bay is secluded and so shallow that the turquoise water glows. Chances are you will be one of only a few on the stunning beach. **Pros:** one of the original villa rentals on Provo has held up well through the years; gorgeous views of Taylor Bay from all the rooms. **Cons:** waterfront but not beachfront; you can only rent Saturday to Saturday; alarm but no on-site security. ⊠ *Ocean Point, Taylor Bay* ⊕*www.TCVillas.com* ➵*5 bedrooms, 5½ baths* ⌂*Safe, dishwasher, DVD, Wi-Fi, weekly maid service, pool, laundry facilities, some pets allowed, no smoking* ▤*No credit cards* ⎮◯⎮*EP* ⌛*1-week min.*

$$$$ 📺**Villa Sublime.** The views from each room of this Silly Creek villa are breathtaking; one side looks out on the endless turquoise of the Caicos Banks, while the other offers views of the neon greens of Chalk Sound. Inside the Spanish-style home every room has an arch, with window seats under huge, arched windows. The infinity pool blends right in with the Caicos Banks, and though the villa is not on the beach, there is a path through the corals to the water. The white-on-white decor is chic, and this is one of only a few villas with a garage. The grill and gorgeous patio were made for entertaining. **Pros:** red roof tiles contrast beautifully with turquoise waters; there are views on all sides of the house. **Cons:** not on a sandy beach; an extra $30 daily charge for air-conditioning; alarm but no on-site security. ✉*Silly Creek Estates, Silly Creek* ☎*649/241–2103* ⊕*www. VillaSublime.com* ⤳*3 bedrooms, 4½ baths* ⚿ *Safe, dishwasher, DVD, Internet, Wi-Fi, weekly maid service, pool, water toys, laundry facilities, no smoking* ⊟*No credit cards* ⏍*EP* ⤶*1- week min.*

BEACHES

You want the best beaches in the world on vacation? That's what you will find in Provo. Everyone comes here for Grace Bay Beach, 12 uninterrupted miles of clean sand with no rocks and unimaginably turquoise water, but you should not overlook Provo's other beaches, each with its own unique allure. You may find it hard to break away from Grace Bay, and while some beaches require some effort to reach, they will reward your effort. On the rare chance that north winds are creating waves on Grace Bay, you can always head to the other side of Provo for guaranteed calm and shallow waters.

★ **Grace Bay** (✉*Grace Bay Rd., on the north shore*), a 12-mi (18-km) sweeping stretch of ivory-white, powder-soft sand on Provo's north coast is simply breathtaking and home to migrating starfish as well as shallow snorkeling trails. The majority of Provo's beachfront resorts are along this shore.

★ **Half Moon Bay** (✉*15 mins from Leeward Marina, between Pine Cay and Water Cay, accessible only by boat*) is a natural ribbon of sand linking two uninhabited cays; it's only inches above the sparkling turquoise waters and one of the most gorgeous beaches on the island. There are limestone cliffs to explore as well as small, private sand coves; there's even a small wreck offshore for snorkeling. It's only a short boat ride away from Provo, and most of the island's tour companies run excursions here or simply offer a beach drop-off. These companies include Silverdeep and Caicos Dream Tours (⇨ *Boating & Sailing, below*).

Long Bay (⊠ *Long Bay Rd.*) is where the sports are. An excellent beach for horseback riding, it's also popular with kite-surfers. If you want to swim here, wear water shoes, as there are many conch shells half-buried in the sand.

Lower Bight Beach (⊠ *Lower Bight Rd., Turtle Cove*) is often confused with Grace Bay Beach because it seems to blend right into it. While the beach is gorgeous, it gets rocky here, offering the best off-the-beach snorkeling—not just in Provo, but possibly the Caribbean.

★ **Fodor'sChoice Malcolm's Beach** (⊠ *Malcolm's Beach Rd., keep straight after passing the Amanyara turn-off*) is one of the most stunning beaches you'll ever see, but you'll need a high-clearance vehicle to reach it. Bring your own food and drinks since there are no facilities or food service unless you have made a reservation with Amanyara to eat at the resort.

Pelican Beach (⊠ *Dolphin Ave., Leeward Going Through*) has the best souvenirs—huge, empty conch shells. Chances are you'll be the only one on this beautiful strand. Because of offshore dredging during the last couple of years, the water is not as crystal-clear as at Grace Bay, but it's an even brighter turquoise.

The best of the many secluded beaches and pristine sands around Provo can be found at **Sapodilla Bay** (⊠ *North of South Dock, at end of South Dock Rd.*), a peaceful quarter-mile cove protected by Sapodilla Hill, with its soft strand lapped by calm waves, where yachts and small boats move with the gentle tide.

Taylor Bay (⊠ *Sunset Dr.*) is shallow for hundreds of yards, making it a perfect place for a private picnic or sunset wedding. Kids become giddy at this beach; they can play in a huge area of chest-high water, and parents don't have to worry about dangerous drop-offs. The beach also offers gorgeous views for the many villas here.

West Harbour Bay (⊠ *Northwest Point*) is a long drive from the heart of Grace Bay, but you'll be rewarded with a stunning, isolated (and technically private) beach. Not only can you find big red starfish in the water here, but you might find a buried pirate's treasure if you correctly interpret the "maps" in the rock carvings. Go while you can; when the Ritz-Carlton development on West Caicos opens for business it will be harder to use this road.

GLOWWORMS. If you're here on the fourth and fifth days after a full moon, you might get to see glowworms. The phenomenon occurs when fluorescent worms mate, then glow in the water like stars twinkling at dusk. The worms will do their dance for about an hour. Sadly, a vibrant phosphorescent show is not guaranteed; some months offer tons of little "stars" in the water; some months are duds with only a few. The best places to view them from land are around the Caicos Banks and Chalk Sound residential neighborhoods. Better yet, see them from an excursion boat.

SPORTS & THE OUTDOORS

BICYCLING

Most hotels have bicycles available for guests, or you can rent one from an independent company. Stick to the sidewalks on Grace Bay Road for safety; drivers don't pay much attention to bikes, and you'll create less dust on this dry island.

Caicos Wheels (⊠ *Queens Landing, Grace Bay* ☎649/242–6592 ⊕ *www.CaicosWheels.com*) offers several options, from scooters and dune buggies to off-road dirt bikes. You can rent mountain bikes at **Scooter Bob's** (⊠*Turtle Cove Marina, Turtle Cove* ☎649/946–4684 ⊕*www.provo.net/ scooter*) for $15 a day.

BOATING & SAILING

Provo's calm, reef-protected seas combine with constant easterly trade winds for excellent sailing conditions. Several multihulled vessels offer charters with snorkeling stops, food and beverage service, and sunset vistas. Prices range from $39 per person for group trips to $600 or more for private charters.

☙ **Beluga Sailboat** (☎649/946–4396 ⊕*www.SailBeluga.com*) offers private charters for six to eight passengers through the cays. Captain Tim knows these waters: he's been sailing for more than two decades. This is true sailing, no motors allowed. Tim will pick you up and take you to the marina on Provo where his boat is moored.

Caicos Dream Tours (☎649/243–3560 ⊕*www.caicosdream tours.com*) offers several snorkeling trips, including one that has you diving for conch before lunch on a gorgeous beach. The company also offers private charters.

For sightseeing below the waves, try the semi-submarine operated by **Caicos Tours** (✉*Turtle Cove Marina, Turtle Cove* ☎649/231–0006 ⊕*www.caicostours.com*). You can stay dry within the small, lower observatory as it glides along on a one-hour tour of the reef, with large viewing windows on either side. The trip costs $39.

Sail Provo (☎649/946–4783 ⊕*www.sailprovo.com*) runs 52-foot and 48-foot catamarans on scheduled half-day, full-day, sunset, and kid-friendly glowworm cruises, where underwater creatures light up the sea's surface for several days after each full moon.

Silverdeep (☎649/946–5612 ⊕*www.silverdeep.com*) sailing trips include time for snorkeling and beachcombing at a secluded beach.

The *Atabeyra,* run by **Sun Charters** (☎649/941–5363 ⊕*www. suncharters.tc*), is a retired rumrunner and the choice of residents for special events.

DIVING & SNORKELING

★ **Fodor**śChoice The island's many shallow reefs offer excellent and exciting snorkeling relatively close to shore. Try **Smith's Reef,** over Bridge Road east of Turtle Cove.

Scuba diving in the crystalline waters surrounding the islands ranks among the best in the Caribbean. The reef and wall drop-offs thrive with bright, unbroken coral formations and lavish numbers of fish and marine life. Mimicking the idyllic climate, waters are warm all year, averaging 76°F to 78°F in winter and 82°F to 84°F in summer. With minimal rainfall and soil runoff, visibility is usually good and frequently superb, ranging from 60 feet to more than 150 feet. An extensive system of marine national parks and boat moorings, combined with an ecoconscious mindset among dive operators, contributes to an uncommonly pristine underwater environment.

Dive operators in Provo regularly visit sites at **Grace Bay** and **Pine Cay** for spur-and-groove coral formations and bustling reef diving. They make the longer journey to the dramatic walls at **North West Point** and **West Caicos** depending on weather conditions. Instruction from the major diving agencies is available for all levels and certifications, even technical diving. An average one-tank dive costs $45; a two-tank dive, $90. There are also two live-aboard dive boats available for charter working out of Provo.

☺ With a certified marine biologist on staff, **Big Blue Unlimited** (✉*Leeward Marina, Leeward* ☎*649/946–5034* ⊕*www.bigblue.tc*) specializes in ecofriendly diving adventures, including special trips for kids involving kayaking through the mangroves or walking along nature trails. It also offers Nitrox and Trimix.

Caicos Adventures (✉*La Petite Pl., Grace Bay* ☎☎*649/941–3346* ⊕*www.tcidiving.com*), run by friendly Frenchman Fifi Kuntz, offers daily trips to West Caicos, French Cay, and Molasses Reef.

Dive Provo (✉*Ports of Call, Grace Bay* ☎*649/946–5040* or *800/234–7768* ⊕*www.diveprovo.com*) is a PADI five-star operation that runs daily one- and two-tank dives to popular Grace Bay sites.

Provo Turtle Divers (✉*Turtle Cove Marina, Turtle Cove* ☎*649/946–4232* or *800/833–1341* ⊕*www.provoturtledivers.com*), which also operates satellite locations at the Ocean Club and Ocean Club West, has been on Provo since the 1970s. The staff is friendly, knowledgeable, and unpretentious.

Snuba Turks & Caicos (✉*Windsong Resort, Stubbs Rd., The Bight* ☎*649/241–7010* ⊕*www.SnubaTurksandCaicos.com*) offers the next-best thing to diving for a noncertified diver; it's completely different from snorkeling but requires no experience. The acronym stands for Surface Nexus Underwater Breathing Apparatus. You can go down to the reef like a scuba diver, but your air tank stays on the surface. Owner Jodie will take a picture of you down below for a keepsake. Children must be at least eight years old to participate.

The **Turks & Caicos Aggressor II** (☎*800/348–2628* ⊕*www.turksandcaicosaggressor.com*), a live-aboard dive boat, plies the islands' pristine sites with weekly charters from Turtle Cove Marina.

FISHING

The islands' fertile waters are great for angling—anything from bottom- and reef-fishing (most likely to produce plenty of bites and a large catch) to bonefishing and deep-sea fishing (among the finest in the Caribbean). Each July the Caicos Classic Catch & Release Tournament attracts anglers from across the islands and the United States who compete to catch the biggest Atlantic blue marlin, tuna, or wahoo. For any fishing activity, you are required to purchase a $15 visitor's fishing license; operators generally furnish all equipment, drinks, and snacks. Prices range from $100 to $375, depending on the length of trip and size of boat.

For deep-sea fishing trips in search of marlin, sailfish, wahoo, tuna, barracuda, and shark, look up **Gwendolyn Fishing Charters** (✉*Turtle Cove Marina, Turtle Cove* ☎*649/946–5321*).

Capt. Arthur Dean at **Silverdeep** (✉*Leeward Marina, Leeward* ☎*649/946–5612 www.silverdeep.com*) is said to be among the Caribbean's finest bonefishing guides.

GOLF

★ **Fodor's**Choice The par-72, 18-hole championship course at **Provo Golf & Country Club** (✉*Governor's Rd., Grace Bay* ☎*649/946–5991* ⊕*www.provogolfclub.com*) is a combination of lush greens and fairways, rugged limestone outcroppings, and freshwater lakes, and is ranked among the Caribbean's top courses. Fees are $160 for 18 holes with shared cart. Premium golf clubs are available.

Turks & Caicos Miniature Golf (✉*Long Bay Rd., Leeward* ☎*649/231–4653*) is open every day and offers free shuttle service to most Grace Bay hotels. A round costs $15, and there is an on-site bar and grill where you can eat after your game.

HORSEBACK RIDING

Provo's beaches and secluded lanes are ideal for trail rides. **Provo Ponies** (☎*649/946–5252* ⊕*www.provo.net/provoponies*) offers morning and afternoon rides for all levels. A 45-minute ride costs $45; an 80-minute ride is $65. The rates include transportation from all major hotels.

Diving the Turks & Caicos Islands

CLOSE UP

Scuba diving was the sport that drew visitors to the Turks and Caicos islands in the 1970s. Aficionados still come for the abundant marine life, including humpback whales in winter, sparkling-clean waters, warm and calm seas, and the coral walls and reefs around the islands. Diving in the Turks and Caicos—especially off Grand Turk, South Caicos, and Salt Cay—is still considered among the best in the world.

Off Providenciales, dive sites are along the north shore's barrier reef. Most sites can be reached in anywhere from 10 minutes to 1½ hours. Dive sites feature spur-and-groove coral formations atop a coral-covered slope. Popular stops like **Aquarium, Pinnacles,** and **Grouper Hole** have large schools of fish, turtles, nurse

sharks, and gray reef sharks. From the south side dive boats go to **French Cay, West Caicos, South West Reef,** and **Northwest Point.** Known for typically calm conditions and clear water, the West Caicos Marine National Park is a favorite stop. The area has dramatic walls and marine life, including sharks, eagle rays, and octopus, with large stands of pillar coral and huge barrel sponges.

Off Grand Turk the 7,000-foot coral-wall **drop-off** is actually within swimming distance of the beach. Buoyed sites along the wall have swim-through tunnels, cascading sand chutes, imposing coral pinnacles, dizzying vertical drops, and undercuts where the wall goes beyond the vertical and fades beneath the reef.

PARASAILING

A 15-minute parasailing flight over Grace Bay is available for $70 (single) or $120 (tandem) from **Captain Marvin's Watersports** (☎*649/231–0643*), who will pick you up at your hotel for your flight. The views as you soar over the bite-shape Grace Bay area, with spectacular views of the barrier reef, are truly unforgettable.

TENNIS

You can rent equipment at **Provo Golf & Country Club** (✉*Grace Bay* ☎*649/946–5991* ⊕*www.provogolfclub.com*) and play on the two lighted courts, which are among the island's best. Nonmembers can play until 5 PM for $10 per hour (reservation required).

WATERSKIING

Nautique Sports offers a water-sports dream. What better place to learn to ski than on the calm, crystal-clear waters of Providenciales? A great company for beginners, Nautique offers private instruction and will have you skiing in no time. Experts can try barefoot skiing. The company also rents kite-surfing equipment. ⊠*Graceway Sportscenter, behind Graceway IGA, Leeward Hwy., Discovery Bay* ☎*649/231–6890* ⊕*www.NautiqueSports.com.*

WINDSURFING

Although the water appears calm, the breezes always blow along Provo's northern shore. Most resorts will provide Windsurfers. If you're on Grace Bay Beach, stay inside the white buoys, boats can pass by beyond them. Nautique Sports also rents kite-surfing equipment (*see Waterskiing, above*).

Windsurfers find the calm, turquoise water of Grace Bay ideal. **Windsurfing Provo** (⊠*Ocean Club, Grace Bay* ☎*649/946–5649* ⊠*Ocean Club West, Grace Bay* ☎*649/231–1687* ⊕*www.windsurfingprovo.tc*) rents kayaks, motorboats, Windsurfers, and Hobie Cats, and offers windsurfing instruction.

SHOPPING

Provo is not really a shopping destination, and you won't find bargains here. However, there is enough upscale shopping to keep your wallet busy, from tropical clothes and jewelry to art prints and accessories. The shopping areas continue to expand; new buildings are being added to Saltmills Plaza and Regent Village. The major resorts have small boutiques with signature items, so don't forget to check them out.

SHOPPING AREAS

There are several main shopping areas in Provo: Grace Bay has the newer **Saltmills** complex and **La Petite Place** retail plaza, the new **Regent Village**, as well as the original **Ports of Call** shopping village. Two markets on the beach near the Ocean Club and the Beaches Turks & Caicos Resort & Spa allow for barefoot shopping.

Local souvenirs

What should you bring home after a fabulous vacation in the Turks and Caicos islands? Here are a few suggestions, some of which are free!

If you comb Pelican Beach or go on a conch-diving excursion, bring two conch shells (the maximum number allowed) home. Remember, only the shell, no living thing, is allowed.

The Middle Caicos Coop shop in Blue Hills sells carved wooden boats from Middle Caicos, and local straw hats and bags. You'll find locally made ceramics at Art Provo and at Turks & Caicos National Trust (at Town Center Mall or next to Island Scoop Ice Cream).

There are two cultural centers, one between Ocean Club East and Club Med, and the other next to Beaches Resort (there's a third one under construction between Aquamarine Beach Houses and the new Gansevoort). Here you'll find batik clothing and locally made jewelry. Custom-made pieces can be ordered.

The Conch Farm sells beautiful, affordable jewelry made from conch shells and freshwater pearls.

One of the best souvenirs is the hardcover coffee-table cookbook from the Red Cross. Not only is it gorgeous, featuring recipes from all the great chefs of the Turks and Caicos, but the proceeds help the Red Cross.

The best free souvenir—besides your phenomenal tan—is a potcake puppy. The puppy you adopt comes with carrier, papers, and all the shots—and will remind you year after year of your terrific vacation.

Handwoven straw baskets and hats, polished conch-shell crafts, paintings, wood carvings, model sailboats, handmade dolls, and metalwork are crafts native to the islands and nearby Haiti. The natural surroundings have inspired local and international artists to paint, sculpt, print, craft, and photograph; most of their creations are on sale in Providenciales.

SPECIALTY STORES

ART & CRAFT GALLERIES

★ **Anna's Art Gallery & Studio** (☒*The Saltmills, Grace Bay* ☏*449/231–3293*) sells original artworks, silk-screen paintings, sculptures, and handmade sea-glass jewelry.

ArtProvo (☒*Regent Village, Grace Bay* ☏*649/941–4545*) is the island's largest gallery of designer wall art; also shown are native crafts, jewelry, handblown glass, candles, and other gift items. Featured artists include Trevor Morgan, from Salt Cay, and Dwight Outten.

★ **Bamboo Gallery** (⊠*Leeward Hwy., The Market Place* ☎*649/946–4748*) sells Caribbean art, from vivid Haitian paintings to wood carvings and local metal sculptures, with the added benefit that artists are usually on hand to describe their works.

Greensleeves (⊠*Central Sq., Leeward Hwy., Turtle Cove* ☎*649/946–4147*) offers paintings and pottery by local artists, baskets, jewelry, and sisal mats and bags. The proceeds from sales of works in the Potcake Corner help fund the Potcake Place rescue center for the islands' stray dogs.

BOOKS

If you need to supplement your beach-reading stock or are looking for island-specific materials, visit the **Unicorn Bookstore** (⊠*In front of Graceway IGA Mall, Leeward Hwy., Discovery Bay* ☎*649/941–5458*) for a wide assortment of books and magazines, lots of information and guides about the Turks and Caicos islands and the Caribbean, and a large children's section with crafts, games, and art supplies.

JEWELRY

Alicia Shulman Jewelry (⊠*Boutique at The Somerset Resort, Grace Bay* ☎*649/946–5900* ⊕*www.AliciaShulman.com*) makes handmade, bold, and beautiful jewelry that shows off your tan. Oversized semiprecious pearls, turquoise, and coral stones combine to make a statement. Celebrities have worn pieces from her collection, and pieces have been featured on VH1's "Glam God with Vivica Fox." Shulman's designs are sold at the boutique at the Somerset Resort and at Parrot Cay.

Cynthia's Jewelry Inspired by Nature's Beauty (⊠ *The Somerset Resort, Grace Bay* ☎*649/946–5900*) makes jewelry by hand from natural stones mixed with Swarovski crystals, incorporated with shells and stars. Not only are the pieces stunning, but all proceeds go to the nonprofit Potcake Place.

Jai's (⊠*Regent Village, Grace Bay* ☎*649/941–4324*) sells diamonds, perfumes, sunglasses, and watches, including the elusive blue diamond, which may remind you of Grace Bay.

Royal Jewels (⊠*Providenciales International Airport* ☎*649/941–4513* ⊠*Arch Plaza* ☎*649/946–4699* ⊠*Beaches Turks & Caicos Resort & Spa, Grace Bay* ☎*649/946–8285* ⊠*Club Med Turkoise, Grace Bay* ☎*649/946–5602*) sells gold and other jewelry, designer watches, perfumes, fine leather goods, and cameras—all duty-free—at several outlets.

CLOTHING FOR WOMEN

Caicos Wear Boutique (⊠*La Petite Pl., Grace Bay Rd., Grace Bay* ☎*649/941–3346*) is filled with casual resort wear, including Caribbean-print shirts, swimsuits from Brazil, sandals, beach jewelry, and gifts.

Ventura Boutique (⊠*Saltmills Plaza, Grace Bay Rd., Grace Bay* ☎*649/941–7793*) carries all the colorful brands you would want to wear in the tropics, including Fresh Produce, Jams World, and Lily Pulitzer.

FOOD

Grocery shopping in Provo is almost as good as at home, with all the American, British, and Canadian brands you crave. Because everything has to be flown in, expect to pay 25% to 50% more than for similar purchases in the United States. Even many hard-to-find products and special dietary foods can be found on Provo. Shipments come in on Sunday, so Monday is your best food-shopping bet.

Beer is expensive, rum is cheaper, and stores are prohibited by law from selling alcohol on Sunday. While it's tempting to bring in your own cooler of food, remember that some airlines charge for checked bags, and there is the risk of losing luggage. More than likely, if it's allowed in the States, it's allowed in Provo—meat, fish, and vegetables can be brought in if frozen and vacuum-sealed; always ask your airline if you will be allowed to check or bring a cooler. If you're traveling for more than a week, then you may save enough money by bringing provisions here to make it worth the trouble. But if you're staying on Provo, there will be no problem buying anything you need.

Cost Right (⊠*Leeward Hwy., Discovery Bay* ☎*649/941–5424*) is smaller than Graceway IGA, but it can be a helpful stop if IGA runs out of certain items.

Gourmet Goods (⊠*Grace Bay Court, Grace Bay Rd., Grace Bay* ☎*649/941–4141* ⊕*www.GourmetGoods.tc*) offers catering for weddings and parties, with spring rolls, smoked salmon, wings and chicken satay trays, prepared foods such as meat loaf and lasagna, and hard-to-find specialty spices and sauces. The storefront has ready-made lunch specials and paninis, tuna salad, and grilled-chicken sandwiches; you can also hire a chef from the company to cook full meals at your home, condo, or villa. For a premium, the company will deliver groceries, snacks, drinks, and fruit to wherever you are staying.

Including a large fresh-produce section, bakery, gourmet deli, and extensive meat counter, **Graceway IGA Supermarket** (⊠*Leeward Hwy., Discovery Bay* ☎*649/941–5000*), Provo's largest, is likely to have what you're looking for, and it's the most consistently well-stocked store on the island. It's got a good selection of prepared foods, including rotisserie chicken, pizza, and potato salad. But prices can be much higher than at home.

Island Pride (⊠*Town Centre Mall, Leeward Hwy., Airport* ☎*649/946–4211*) has a good selection of everything you need, plus an additional Digicel phone outlet. This often-overlooked supermarket carries all the name brands you would seek.

Kissing Fish Catering Co. (⊠*Grace Bay Rd., at Bay Bistro, Grace Bay* ☎*649/941–8917* ⊕*www.KissingFish.tc*) has the same owners as Bay Bistro and Aqua Bar and Terrace. The company will cater events like full-moon bonfires on the beach, weddings, and private parties, including beachside romantic dinners for two. Choose from pig roasts and ribs to four-course meals with beef Wellington, grouper with mango chutney, grilled lobster, or grilled chicken with sun-dried tomatoes, just to name a few from the extensive menu. If you're staying in a villa or condo with full kitchen, you can hire a personal chef to prepare meals in your kitchen.

HOME DECOR

Inter Decor (⊠*Saltmills Plaza, Grace Bay* ☎*649/941–8717*) is a popular island interior-design store, where you can find tropical shells, bookends, and fish vases.

LIQUOR

For a large selection of duty-free liquor, visit **Discount Liquors** (⊠*Leeward Hwy., east of Suzie Turn Rd., Turtle Cove* ☎*649/946–4536*).

SOUVENIRS

Mama's (⊠ *Ports of Call Shopping Center, Grace Bay Rd., Grace Bay* ☎649/946–5538) is the place for typical souvenirs and trinkets; you can also get your hair braided here. What really makes shopping fun is Mama herself, who may decide to sing a song or dance.

Silverdeep Boutique (⊠ *Grace Bay Plaza, Grace Bay Rd., Grace Bay* ☎649/946–5612 ⊕*www.Silverdeep.com*) not only does excursions well but also has an awesome boutique. Tropical shirts, bathing suits, and sandals are just a small part of what the store carries; here you can buy carvings from the "Conch Man."

NIGHTLIFE

While Provo is not known for its nightlife, there's still some fun to be had after dark. On Friday nights you can start off by dancing in the sand at Da Conch Shack (⇨*Where to Eat, above)*, then you can listen to one of the live bands that plays at Calico Jack's. Thursday-night and Saturday-night hot spots include Danny Buoy's. On Saturday nights at Turks & Caicos Miniature Golf Fun World, you can play a round, sing karaoke, and dance the night away all in one spot (⇨*Golf, above*). Be sure to see if any ripsaw bands—aka rake-and-scrape—are playing while you're on-island; this is one of the typical types of music on the island.

Late-night action can be found at Nikki Beach, where music plays until the wee hours, and Casablanca Casino, where everyone ends the night. The best ambience is wherever Daniel and Nadine are singing; this crowd-pleasing couple has a following—even among tourists. There's live music on Thursday nights at Da Conch Shack, Friday nights at the patio of O'Soleil, and Sunday nights at Tiki Hut. Now there's a reason to go out on Tuesday; a sunset clam bake at The Somerset offers clams and buckets of beer.

Keep abreast of events and specials by checking **TCI eNews** (⊕*www.tcienews.com*).

FULL MOON PARTIES. Full moons are reputed to make people a little crazy, and two places on Provo offer bonfires on the beach to take advantage of the mood. On the first night of a full moon, Horse-Eyed Jacks has a huge bonfire on the beach in Blue Hills, with ribs and baked beans and dancing on the sand. Bay Bistro usually has one the next night on Grace Bay Beach, with a pig roast and tropical fare such as pineapple coleslaw. Bay Bistro's bonfire is a great hit with the kids, since you can roast marsh-mallows and make s'mores.

RECOMMENDED BARS

On Friday nights you can find a local band and lively crowd at **Calico Jack's Restaurant & Bar** (⊠*Ports of Call, Grace Bay* ☎*649/946–5129*).

The **Casablanca Casino** (⊠*Grace Bay Rd., Grace Bay* ☎*649/941–3737*) has brought slots, blackjack, American roulette, poker, craps, and baccarat back to Provo. Open from 7 PM until 5 AM, this is the last stop for the night. Grace Bay Club has introduced the Infinity Bar, the only one of its kind in the world, which gives the impression it goes directly into the ocean.

A popular gathering spot for locals to shoot pool, play darts, slam dominoes, and catch up on gossip is **Club Sodax Sports Bar** (⊠*Leeward Hwy., Grace Bay* ☎*649/941–4540*). You won't go hungry with snacks such as conch and fish fingers, jerk pork, and typical native dishes.

Danny Buoy's (⊠*Grace Bay Rd., across from Carpe Diem Residences, Grace Bay* ☎*649/946–5921*) is a popular Irish pub, with pool tables, darts and big-screen TVs. It's a great place to watch sports from anywhere in the world.

Junkanoo's Bar & Grill (⊠*Lower Bight Rd., Grace Bay* ☎*649/941–8452*) is a favorite local spot for sports events, movie nights, and endless happy-hour specials.

Nikki Beach (⊠*Leeward Marina, , Leeward Going Through* ☎*649/941–3747*) is now *the* place for nightlife in Provo; it's chic and elegant yet active and fun. On Thursday, Friday, and Saturday, the action starts late here, sometimes after midnight, and can go on into the wee hours of the morning. Beautiful girls dance on the bar while patrons sit on couches and daybeds scattered in the sand under tiki torches.

The Players Club (⊠*Lower Bight Rd., Turtle Cove* ☎*649/941–4263* ⊕*www.ThePlayersClub.tc*) has more than 100 electronic gaming machines but is better known for the live nightly poker games. The casino hosted the "World Poker Tour" in 2007, as seen on The Travel Channel.

SPAS

Except for Parrot Cay, Provo is the best destination in the Turks & Caicos if you are looking or a spa vacation. The spas here offer treatments with all the bells and whistles, and most get very good word of mouth. Most of Provo's high-end resorts have spas, but if you're staying at a villa, Spa Tropique will come to you.

Anani Spa at Grace Bay Club (✉ *Villas at Grace Bay Club, Grace Bay* ☎*649/946–5050* ⊕*www.gracebayclub.com*) is on the Villas side of the complex; the six treatment rooms have alfresco showers, but treatments can also be performed on your balcony at Grace Bay Club facing the ocean. One of the most popular treatments is the Exotic Lime and Ginger Salt Glow; not only will it polish your skin, but the aroma it leaves on your skin is worth the treatment.

Beaches Red Line Spa (✉ *Beaches Turks & Caicos Resort & Spa, Lower Bight Rd., Grace Bay* ☎*649/946–8000* ⊕*www. beaches.com*) is open to nonresort guests. It has one hot plunge pool and one cold plunge pool to get the circulation going. During special hours, it offers kid's treatments, too. Although Beaches is an all-inclusive resort, spa treatments are an additional charge to guests.

Como Shambhala at Parrot Cay (✉ *Parrot Cay* ☎*649/946–7788* ⊕*shambhala.como.bz*) has extensive retreat facilities and has thought of everything you might need for your mind, body, and soul. Treatments run the gamut from Asian holistic treatments to yoga with the world's leading teachers in a stunning pavilion to a signature health-conscious cuisine. The infinity pool, Pilates studio, steam room, sauna, and outdoor Jacuzzi make you feel complete. If you're staying in Provo, you can call for reservations, but you must pay for the boat ride to Parrot Cay. It's reputed to be one of the finest spas in the world, and you'd be hard-pressed to find a better one in the Turks and Caicos.

Regent Spa (✉ *Regent Palms, Grace Bay* ☎*649/946–8666* ⊕*www.regenthotels.com*) is so gorgeous that it has been featured on countless travel magazine covers. A reflecting pool with majestic date palms sets the ambience. The signature treatment, a "Mother of Pearl Body Exfoliation," uses hand-crushed local conch shells to revitalize and soften skin. On an island already boasting several terrific spas, the combination of the beautiful setting and treatments incorporating local ingredients makes this a standout.

2

Spa Sanay (⊠*Grace Bay Court, Grace Bay Rd., Grace Bay* ☎*649/946–8212*), an independent spa in a small shopping center on Grace Bay Road, offers treatments at 50% off for children, so that they may also enjoy the spa. With a full line of services, it's a great place to have your hair and nails done for weddings. One of the signature services is ear candling, which reduces ear pressure and can relieve headaches.

Spa Tropique (⊠ *Ports of Call Shopping Center, Grace Bay Rd. Grace Bay* ☎*649/331–2040* ⊕*www.SpaTropique. com*) is unique on Provo for its mobile service. You pick the setting, and the spa comes to you—an ideal option for those in more isolated villas who can't bear to leave their island paradise; the spa can also come to your hotel room (provided your hotel has no spa of its own). Have your treatment on your balcony, or on the beach or by the pool, which will make the treatments seem extra special. Spa Tropique's one-of-a-kind Turks Island Salt Glow incorporates local salts from Grand Turk and Salt Cay. The spa also has locations at Ocean Club West and The Sands Resort.

Teona Spa (⊠*Villa Renaissance, Grace Bay* ☎*649/941–5051* ⊕*www.TheRegentGrandResort.com*) caters to both Villa Renaissance and the Regent Grand Resort with treatment such as the "Two Hot to Handle" couples massage. The therapists keep you in unison with a warming Boreh mask and Mediterranean hot-oil massage. Afterwards you can wind down with spice tea or a glass of wine.

Thalasso Spa at Point Grace (⊠*Point Grace, Grace Bay* ☎*649/946–5096, Ext. 4129* ⊕*www.pointgrace.com*) has three whitewashed open-air cabanas on the dunes looking out to the beach. French skin oils and the latest European techniques are incorporated in all skin treatments, along with elements of the ocean, including sea mud, seaweed, and sea salt. The setting alone, with the breezes and views of Grace Bay, is worth the stop.

WEST CAICOS

West Caicos is rich in history; pirates have hidden out here, using the island to ambush their enemies. One of the largest Spanish-galleon treasures was found in the waters that surround West Caicos. There's a rumor that Christopher Columbus's ship, the *Pinta*, is at the bottom of the sea here. West Caicos has the most attractive natural landscape of any island in the Turks and Caicos, with silver palms and ponds hosting bright-pink flamingos. There are old cotton-plantation ruins to explore. There are cliffs from which you can dive.

The best scuba diving in the area immediately surrounding Provo takes place in these waters; the corals drop off to more than 6,000 feet. So dramatic and instant is the drop-off that the water appears to be deep purple. Providenciales dive outfitters take divers to West Caicos as the premier dive location.

But you have only three ways to come and enjoy West Caicos: via your own boat, with a dive company, or by staying at Molasses Reef Resort (when it's completed).

Molasses Reef Resort, a Ritz-Carlton–managed property, will fill the entire island. A private yacht takes you on the 20-minute ride to paradise. The Bermudian and Old Caribbean architecture consists of huge patios and balconies with palm fans and gentle breezes, all facing a spectacular beach. This will certainly be one of Ritz-Carlton's top properties in the Caribbean when completed. Each villa will have its own staff, who will live in buildings on the property so that they are always nearby and available. Each guest will be given an electric golf cart for exploring the island. For the few who can afford it, this will be a tremendous experience.

The Caicos and the Cays

WORD OF MOUTH

"A boat excursion to nearby cays was my favorite thing to do in T&C. The beaches there are beautiful."

—Caribtraveler

By
Ramona
Settle

VERY FEW VISITORS TO THE Turks and Caicos venture out from Provo, but when they do, they discover a whole other side to islands. Most of the outlying cays are uninhabited, yet offer much for the adventurous explorer. You can also find cays that were pirate hideaways in the 17th and 18th centuries, now with resorts that take up the entire island. Most cays can be explored on day trips from Provo. The cays have endless beaches that you might have to yourself, with hidden coves where you can picnic while watching the boats go by, and many have small limestone cliffs with endless views of the ocean. Many are inhabited by friendly iguanas and circled by stingrays; if you are lucky, JoJo the dolphin might even swim with you. Surrounded by coral reefs, these waters were made for snorkeling, and the many reefs keep waves from crashing on shore, keeping the water calm like a lagoon. You can find cannons under the water and sand dollars to bring back home. South, North, and Middle Caicos offer a step back in time to rustic, lazy days in the sun. Pine Cay is rustic yet refined, laid-back yet charming. Parrot Cay was made for pampering, a day in the life of a movie star.

ABOUT THE HOTELS
Accommodations here are generally either in the budget category or very expensive, and you won't find very many in the middle price ranges. You'll find several rustic, basic hotels and villas in South, North, and Middle Caicos; the owners are pleasant and helpful, and the towns are small and charming. All are clean and comfortable and offer air-conditioning, satellite TV, and home-cooked meals—everything that you could need to get away from it all. At the other end of the spectrum is pure pampering. Pine Cay is like a luxury camp, quiet and relaxing, with a clubby atmosphere. Parrot Cay is one of the finest resorts in the world, where every need is anticipated and met—sorbet and cold bottled water by the pool and beach are placed in your hands seemingly before you even think about them. Throw in the best spa in the world, and relaxing doesn't get better than this.

ABOUT THE RESTAURANTS
The outer islands don't offer much in the way of independent restaurants, and each island has only a handful of places to eat. Most of the Caicos Islands restaurants base menus on what was caught that day; some eating establishments are in private homes. You must call ahead—if you just show up, you might not get fed. The food in most of

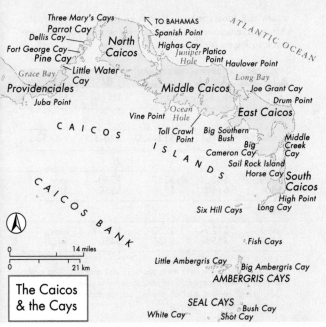

these places is simple island fare, served either in an indoor dining room or on an outdoor patio—often in the chef's own home. At Pine Cay food is included in your room rate, and the pool and beach setting combined with an outdoor grill make for fine casual meals. Parrot Cay, a private island retreat, has two elegant and upscale restaurants for guests to choose from. With advance reservations it's possible for nonguests to eat lunch at Pine Cay and Parrot Cay. Lunch will be expensive, but many travelers find that it's worth it for the chance to visit.

PLANNING YOUR TIME

It's easy to do a bit of exploring on your own by car. Start your day by taking the early ferry from Walkin Marina to North Caicos. Rent a car there to explore both North and Middle Caicos, which are connected by a causeway. From North Caicos marina there is only one long road; with stops, the trip from one end of the island to the other can take a couple of hours. You can stop and snorkel at Three Mary Cays then eat lunch at Silver Palms and observe the laid-back, sleepy life of another era. Stop at Flamingo Pond to count those large, pink birds. Check out the bonefish flats on the way to Middle Caicos. Stop at the Middle Caicos caves and look for bats, then hike the trails of the cliffs. After your sojourn to this peaceful world, you can head back to Provo for dinner.

WHAT IT COSTS IN U.S. DOLLARS				
¢	$	$$	$$$	$$$$
RESTAURANTS				
under $8	$8–$12	$12–$20	$20–$30	over $30
HOTELS*				
under $80	$80–$150	$150–$250	$250–$350	over $350
HOTELS**				
under $125	$125–$250	$250–$350	$350–$450	over $450

*EP, BP, CP **AI, FAP, MAP
Restaurant prices are for a main course at dinner and include any taxes or service charges. Hotel prices are per night for a double room in high season, excluding taxes, service charges, and meal plans (except at all-inclusives).

LITTLE WATER CAY

5 minutes by boat from Walkin' or Leeward marina.

☾ This small, uninhabited cay is a protected area under the
★ Turks & Caicos National Trust and just a stone's throw away from Walkin' and Leeward marinas. On a private boat, the trip takes five minutes; an excursion boat takes five to 15 minutes once you leave the Grace Bay area. On these 150 acres are two trails, small lakes, red mangroves, and an abundance of native plants. Boardwalks protect the ground, and interpretive signs explain the habitat. The small island is home to about 2,000 rare, endangered rock iguanas. Experts say the iguanas are shy, but these creatures actually seem rather curious. They waddle right up to you, as if posing for a picture. Several water-sports operators from Provo and North Caicos include a stop on the island as a part of a snorkel or sailing excursion (it's usually called Iguana Island). There's a $5 permit fee to visit the cay, and the proceeds go toward conservation in the islands.
⚠ **Unless you're a woman who loves to get a pedicure the hard way, watch your toes when you are standing in sand near the**

TOP REASONS TO GO

Day excursions. All of Provo's excursion companies offer trips out to the cays. You can snorkel the reef, check out the iguanas at Little Water Cay, have a barbecue lunch on a secluded beach, and dive for conch all in one afternoon. On a full-day excursion you can go as far as Middle Caicos, where you can hike trails and explore caves. Keep an eye out for JoJo, the dolphin that's the unofficial mascot of Turks and Caicos and who may decide to join you.

Parrot Cay. Live like a rock star, if only for a day. Reservations are mandatory and not guaranteed, but if you can get here for lunch it's oh-so worth it—extravagant, but worth every penny. Lunch guests get access to the gorgeous beach, pool, and one of the best spas in the world.

Pine Cay. If you need to forget the worries of the day, this is your place. Call Le Meridian Club to set up the boat ride and lunch. Everything here is rustic and charming, laid-back and relaxing, and the beach is one of the best.

Scuba South Caicos. South Caicos is all about diving, as it's surrounded by coral walls that start at 30 feet and drop to more than 7,000 feet. The visibility here is the trump card: it's the best in the Turks and Caicos. Since you can't fly and dive on the same day, why not take full advantage of your dive and overnight here?

iguanas—they have been known to mistake partially buried colored nails for grapes!

GETTING THERE

The only way to reach Little Water Cay is by organized excursion or private boat.

PINE CAY

15 to 20 minutes by boat from Provo.

Pine Cay's 2½-mi-long (4-km-long) beach is among the most beautiful in the archipelago. The 800-acre private island, which is in the string of small cays between Provo and North Caicos, is home to a secluded resort and almost 40 private residences. The beach alone is reason to stay here: the sand seems a little whiter, the water a little brighter than beaches on the other cays. Nonguests of the Meridien Club can make reservations for lunch, which will include the private boat transfer. Expect to pay between $100 and $150 for the day; there are themed buffets on Sunday.

GETTING THERE

The only way to reach Pine Cay is by private boat or on the Meridian Club resort's private ferry. If you're a guest of the resort and are staying for a week, one round-trip on the private shuttle is included in your rates. The price you will be quoted for lunch changes daily, and does not include drinks. There is no schedule for the boat: it operates as needed.

Contacts Meridian Club (☎649/946–7758 ⊕ www.Meridian Club.com).

WHERE TO STAY

For approximate costs, see the dining and lodging price chart at the beginning of this chapter.

★ Fodor's Choice ☒ **Meridian Club.** You might feel unplugged when
$$$$ you step onto Pine Cay, since there is no TV, telephone, or traffic to be found on the tiny private island. The charm of this resort, which was built in the 1970s, is that it never changes; it prides itself on simplicity rather than celebrity. The simple beachfront cottages, most of the staff, and what is perhaps the world's smallest airport (in truth, a gazebo) have all stayed the same. On some nights, you can drive your golf cart to the runway for drive-in movie night. The 2½-mi (4-km) stretch of beach is deserted, and instead of roads you find nature trails and sun-dappled paths that crisscross the island, which can be explored by bike or on foot. Cuisine is excellent, with fresh seafood and delicious cakes and tarts served at lunch, dinner, and afternoon tea. Guests are mostly overstressed executives, mature couples, and honeymooners; a large percentage of guests are repeat visitors. Children are welcome only in June and July. **Pros:** the finest beach in Turks and Caicos; rates include of some of the best food in the Turks and Caicos as well as snorkel trips. **Cons:** no TVs or phones, so you are really unplugged here. ⊠*Pine Cay* ☎*649/946–7758 or 866/746–3229* ⊕*www.meridianclub.com* ⇆*12 rooms, 1 cottage, 7 villas* ⚷*In-room: no a/c, no phone, no TV. In-hotel: restaurant, room service, bar, tennis court, pool, beachfront, water sports, bicycles, laundry service, Internet terminal, no kids under 12* ▤*AE, D, MC, V* ⊗*Closed Aug.–Oct.* ⦿*AI.*

FORT GEORGE CAY

15 to 20 minutes by boat from Leeward Marina.

An uninhabited cay and a protected national park, Fort George Cay was once a fortified island that protected the surrounding waters from pirates. Cannons put in place during the 19th century are underwater here and can be viewed by snorkelers. The beach is stunning, a photographer's delight; the curved shoreline creates swirls of different shades of turquoise in the water; at low tide sandbars appear, and the blue-and-green water looks even brighter. This is a great spot to search for sand dollars, so bring a cookie tin to bring them back home in. You can only collect white sand dollars; gray or dark ones are alive and illegal to take. All the excursion companies make stops here, so ask if the island is on the itinerary of the boat you plan to take, either for snorkeling or a beach picnic.

GETTING THERE
The only way to reach Fort George Cay is by organized excursion or private boat.

DELLIS CAY

20 minutes by boat from Leeward Marina.

This stunning small island, the second-to-last cay in the string of small islands between Providenciales and North Caicos, has a gorgeous sandy beach and good snorkeling; it's also a good place to search for sand dollars. It's currently uninhabited, but ground has been broken for a new Mandarin Oriental resort here, which will be an ultradeluxe resort with exclusive villas. As you pass by the building site, you can see piles of sand and construction activity. This small island used to make a great stop, but because of the dredging, the water here is now cloudy. When construction levels off in a year or two, the snorkeling should once again be glorious.

GETTING THERE
At this writing the only way to reach Dellis Cay is by private boat; excursion companies don't stop here anymore.

Good Beach Reads

Consider taking one of these books on your island vacation—it might amuse or even inspire you.

■ *A Trip to the Beach,* by Melinda Blanchard and Robert Blanchard, is about the adventures of opening their dream restaurant in paradise—in this case, a paradise called Anguilla.

■ *Don't Stop the Carnival: A Novel,* by Herman Wouk—who may be better known for his more serious novel *The Winds of War* or his play *The Caine Mutiny Court Martial*—is a comedy about living out your dreams on a tropical island.

■ *An Embarrassment of Mangos: A Caribbean Interlude,* by Ann Vanderhoof, follows a couple sailing through and surviving the Bahamas.

■ *The Carnival Never Got Started,* by S. Guy Lovelace, tells the tales and hardships of building a dream resort on an isolated island. The island is Salt Cay; the resort is the recently shuttered Windmills Plantation. The book is a haunting read, now that Hurricane Ike destroyed the colorful buildings.

PARROT CAY

20 minutes by boat from Provo.

The last in a string of small islands between Providenciales and North Caicos, Parrot Cay was once a hideout for pirate Calico Jack Rackham and his lady cohorts Mary Read and Anne Bonny. The 1,000-acre cay, between Fort George Cay and North Caicos, is now the site of an ultra-exclusive hideaway resort. If you're lucky enough to stay here, you'll have endless beautiful beaches and some small ruins to explore. Originally called Pirate Cay (because of the Spanish galleon treasures believed to be buried somewhere on the island), the island's name was changed to Parrot Cay when the resort was built.

Non-guests may eat lunch at the Lotus restaurant. Reservations are mandatory and may not be available during the busy periods, but if you go, it's a great day. And you may also visit the spa and pool.

GETTING THERE

The only way to reach Parrot Cay is by private boat or the resort's private ferry from a private dock. If you are staying on Provo and would like to go to Parrot Cay for lunch or spa treatments, you must make a reservation and pay for your trip. The private ferry to Parrot Cay runs only for guests and resort workers returning home to Provo. With a reservation, your name will be added to the passenger list.

Contacts **Parrot Cay** (☎649/946–7788 ⊕www.ParrotCay.como.bz).

WHERE TO STAY

For approximate costs, see the dining and lodging price chart at the beginning of this chapter.

3

★ **Fodor's**Choice 🏨 **Parrot Cay Resort.** This private paradise—a
$$$$ favorite of celebrities and other jet-setters—comes with all the trimmings you'd expect for the price. Elaborate ocean-front villas border the island, and their wooden, Asian feel contrasts with the hillside terra-cotta–and–stucco building that houses the spacious suites. Suite and villa interiors are a minimalist yet sumptuous mix of cool-white interiors, Indonesian furnishings, and four-poster beds. The villas are the ultimate indulgence, with heated lap pools, hot tubs, and butler service. The resort's main pool is surrounded by a round, thatched bar and the Asian-inspired Lotus restaurant. The giant Como Shambhala Spa takes destination spas to a whole new level with Indonesian and Balinese therapists. Car transfers to and from the airport and one round-trip by boat to and from the island are included; guests will be met at the airport by a Parrot Cay representative. **Pros:** impeccable service; gorgeous secluded beach; the spa is considered one of the best in the region. **Cons:** only two restaurants on the entire island; it can be costly to get back and forth to Provo for excursions, as there is only private ferry service. ⊠*Parrot Cay* 🖃*Box 164, Providenciales* ☎*649/946–7788* ⊕*www.parrotcay.como. bz* 🛏*42 rooms, 4 suites, 14 villas* &*In-room: safe, kitchen (some), refrigerator, DVD (some), Wi-Fi. In-hotel: 2 restaurants, room service, bars, tennis courts, pool, gym, spa, beachfront, water sports, laundry service, Internet terminal, Wi-Fi* ⊟*AE, MC, V* ⦿*BP.*

NORTH CAICOS

Thanks to abundant rainfall, this 41-square-mi (106-square-km) island is the lushest in the Turks and Caicos chain. With an estimated population of only 1,500, the expansive island allows you to get away from it all. Bird lovers can see a

All in the Family

Belongers, from the taxi driver meeting you at the airport to the chef feeding you, are often related. "Oh, him?" you will hear. "He my cousin!" Development has been mercifully slow here, so family connections, as well as crafts, bush medicine, ripsaw music, storytelling, and recipes, have remained constant. But where do such traditions come from? Recently, researchers came closer to finding out. Many Belongers had claimed that their great-great-grandparents had told them their forebears had come directly from Africa. For decades these stories were ignored. Indeed, most experts believed that Belongers were descendants of mostly second-generation Bermudian and Caribbean slaves.

In 2005 museum researchers continued their search for a lost slave ship called *Trouvadore*. The ship, which was wrecked off East Caicos in 1841, carried a cargo of 193 Africans, captured to be sold into slavery, almost all of whom miraculously survived the wreck. As slavery had been abolished in this British territory at the time, all the Africans were found and freed in the Turks and Caicos islands. With only a few thousand inhabitants in the islands, these first-generation African survivors comprised about 7% of the population. Researchers have concluded that all the Belongers today may be linked by blood or marriage to this one incident.

During one expedition, divers found a wrecked ship of the right time period. If these remains are *Trouvadore*, the Belongers may finally have a physical link to their past to go with their cultural traditions. So while you're in the islands, look closely at the intricately woven baskets, listen carefully to the African rhythms in the ripsaw music, and savor the stories you hear. They may very well be the legacy of *Trouvadore* speaking to you from the past. For more information, check out ⊕*www. slaveshiptrouvadore.com.*

large flock of flamingos here; anglers can find shallow creeks full of bonefish; and history buffs can visit the ruins of a Loyalist plantation. Although there's little traffic, almost all the roads are paved, so bicycling is an excellent way to sightsee. The island could become one of the region's next tourism hot spots, and foundations have been laid for condo resorts such as St. Charles on Horse Stable Beach and Royal Reef Resort at Sandy Point. Even though it's a quiet place, you can find some small eateries around the airport and in Whitby, giving you a chance to try local and seafood specialties, sometimes served with homegrown okra or corn. The beaches are more natural here, and they are sometimes covered with seaweed and pine needles, as there are no major resorts to rake them daily. Nevertheless, some of these secluded strands are breathtaking, even if not as manicured as those of the upscale resorts on Provo.

PHOTOGRAPHY TIP. **Don't you hate finding that your pictures lack the bright colors you saw at the beach and on the water? Brightly lit water reflects on the lens and causes the pictures to look washed out. Solution? Use a circular polarizer—it's like sunglasses for your camera, reducing glare and saturating colors so your pictures look professional.**

GETTING THERE

You can reach North Caicos from Provo with a daily ferry from Walkin Marina in Leeward; the trip takes about 30 minutes. If you rent a car on North Caicos, you can even drive on the new causeway to Middle Caicos, a great day trip from Provo.

Contacts **Caribbean Cruisin'** (⊠ *Walkin Marina, Leeward, Providenciales* ☎ *649/946–5406 or 649/231–4191* ⊕ *tcimall.tc/northcaicos/ images/ferryservice.pdf*).

EXPLORING NORTH CAICOS

Flamingo Pond. This is a regular nesting place for the beautiful pink birds. They tend to wander out in the middle of the pond, so bring binoculars to get a better look.

Kew. This settlement has a small post office, a school, a church, and ruins of old plantations—all set among lush tropical trees bearing limes, papayas, and custard apples. Visiting Kew will give you a better understanding of the daily life of many islanders.

Three Mary Cays. Three small rocks within swimming distance from Whitby Beach give you some of the best secluded snorkeling in all of the Turks and Caicos. You will often find ospreys nesting here, making this area a bird-lover's dream. ⊠ *Off Whitby Beach*.

🕓 **Wades Green.** Visitors can view well-preserved ruins of the great house, overseer's house, and surrounding walls of one of the most successful plantations of the Loyalist era. A lookout tower provides views for miles. Contact the

Coming Attractions

CLOSE UP

The buzz about Turks and Caicos has increased steadily since the turn of the millennium, a fact that hasn't missed the ears of developers. **Gansevoort Turks & Caicos** will bring modern chic to Grace Bay, while **Veranda** offers a landscape of pastel-colored clapboard villas. **Vista Azul** and **Seafeathers** are nearly complete, and will add places to stay in the Turtle Cove section of Provo. Ground has been broken on **Tuscana**, which will bring a little bit of Italy to the Caribbean; **The Shore Club** will be the only resort on Long Bay.

One of the most eagerly anticipated projects on the island is the new water park at **Beaches**, one of the largest in the Caribbean, with slides, lazy rivers, and wave action, which opened earlier in 2009; it complements the new Italian Village that Beaches launched in 2009.

Given the volume of construction going on in Provo now, it's worth asking your hotel about any nearby projects and the noise, dust, and obstructed views that can sometimes result.

National Trust for tour details. ✉*Kew* ☎*649/941–5710 for National Trust* ☝*$5* ☉*Daily, by appointment only.*

WHERE TO STAY

For approximate costs, see the dining and lodging price chart at the beginning of this chapter.

$$ 🖫 **Bottle Creek Lodge.** Colorful, self-contained bungalows
🗘 are scattered close to the water, providing a get-away-from-it-all feeling. Although this small resort is not close to the best beaches of North Caicos, it's the perfect place for fishing and relaxing. Bonefishing is right outside your door; the owners have motorboats available for deep-sea fishing. You'll be welcomed as if you are coming home, and the restaurant has some of the best food on the island. It's possible to use Paypal if you don't have a credit card for payment. **Pros:** very colorful and peaceful; great fishing. **Cons:** not close to the best beaches in North Caicos; requires a car. ✉*Belmont* ☎*649/946–7080* ⊕*www.bottlecreeklodge. com* ➬*3 rooms* ⚑*In-room: kitchen, no phone, no TV, Wi-Fi. In-hotel: restaurant, room service, bar, water sports, bicycles, laundry service, Internet terminal, some pets allowed, no-smoking rooms* ☰*MC, V* ☉⎮*EP.*

$-$$ ☑ **Ocean Beach Hotel & Condominiums.** On Whitby Beach, this horseshoe-shaped, two-story, solar-paneled resort offers ocean views, comfortable and neatly furnished apartments, and a freshwater pool at quite reasonable rates. The Silver Palm restaurant is a welcome addition to the on-site amenities, which also include a dive and water-sports operation called Beach Cruiser. Unit 5 has the best views over the beach—especially for honeymooners, who automatically receive a 10% discount. You pay extra for air-conditioning, however. **Pros:** on the best beach of North Caicos. **Cons:** you need a car to get anywhere on North Caicos. ☒ *Whitby* ☎649/946–7113, 800/710–5204, 905/690–3817 *in Canada* ⊕*www.turksandcaicos.tc/oceanbeach* ➩*10 suites* ♿*In-room: kitchen (some), no TV (some). In-hotel: restaurant, bar, pool, beachfront, diving, water sports, bicycles, laundry service, Internet terminal* ⊟*AE, D, MC, V* ⊗*Closed June 15–Oct. 15* ℴ*EP.*

$ ☑ **Pelican Beach Hotel.** North Caicos islanders Susan and Clifford Gardiner built this small, palmetto-fringed hotel in the 1980s on the quiet, mostly deserted Whitby Beach. The couple's friendliness and insights into island life, not to mention Susan's home-baked bread and island dishes (Cliff's favorite is her cracked conch and island lobster), are the best features. Over the years upkeep of the property has been somewhat inconsistent, but rooms are nevertheless comfortable. Best are the cottage-style rooms (numbered 1 through 6), which are exactly five steps from the windswept beach. **Pros:** the beach is just outside your room. **Cons:** at this writing rooms are still in the very slow process of being renovated and updated. ☒ *Whitby* ☎649/946–7112 ⊕*www.pelicanbeach.tc* ➩*14 rooms, 2 suites* ♿*In-room: no phone, no TV. In-hotel: restaurant, bar, beachfront, bicycles, water sports* ⊟*MC, V* ⊗*Closed Aug. 15–Sept. 15* ℴ*MAP.*

BEACHES

The beaches of North Caicos are superb for shallow snorkeling and sunset strolls, and the waters offshore have excellent scuba diving. **Horse Stable Beach** is the main beach for annual events and beach parties and has the luxurious St. Charles Resort. **Whitby Beach** usually has a gentle tide, and its thin strip of sand is bordered by palmetto plants and taller trees. **Sandy Point** is a gorgeous strand, now taken over by Royal Reef Resort construction. Most of the strands have no development on them, leaving the beaches in a more natural state.

MIDDLE CAICOS

At 48 square mi (124 square km) and with fewer than 300 residents, this is the largest yet least developed of the inhabited islands in the Turks and Caicos chain. A limestone ridge runs to about 125 feet above sea level, creating dramatic cliffs on the north shore and a cave system farther inland. Middle Caicos has rambling trails along the coast; the Crossing Place Trail, which is maintained by the National Trust, follows the path used by the early settlers to go between the islands. Inland are quiet settlements with friendly residents.

North Caicos and Middle Caicos are now linked by a causeway, so it's possible to take a ferry from Provo to North Caicos, rent a car, and explore both North Caicos and Middle Caicos in a single day.

GETTING THERE

The only way to reach Middle Caicos is by car (over the causeway that connects it to North Caicos) or on a flight with Air Turks & Caicos.

Airline Contacts Air Turks & Caicos (☎649/941–5481 ⊕www. airturksandcaicos.com).

EXPLORING MIDDLE CAICOS

♻ **Conch Bar Caves.** These limestone caves have eerie underground lakes and milky-white stalactites and stalagmites. Archaeologists have discovered Lucayan Indian artifacts in the caves and the surrounding area. The caves are inhabited by some harmless bats. If you visit, don't worry—they don't bother visitors. It's best to get a guide. If you tour the caves, be sure to wear sturdy shoes, not sandals.

WHERE TO STAY

For approximate costs, see the dining and lodging price chart at the beginning of this chapter.

$$ ⊠ **Blue Horizon Resort.** At this resort undulating cliffs skirt one of the most dramatic beaches in the Turks and Caicos. Blue-tin roofs mark the small, self-contained open-plan cottages. Screened-in porches and careful positioning ensure that all of the cottages have unobstructed views along the

cliffs and out to sea. The lack of amenities and development is actually what makes this spot so special. Tropical Cottage has large, attractive murals; Dragon View Cottage has spectacular views of Dragon Cay and is closest to the Crossing Place trail that winds along the cliff tops. **Pros:** breathtaking views of Mudjin Harbor from the rooms; lack of amenities and development make you feel like you're away from it all. **Cons:** lack of amenities and development; may be too isolated for some. ⊠*Mudjin Harbor, Conch Bar* ☎*649/946–6141* ⊕*www.bhresort.com* ⇦*5 cottages, 2 villas* ⚲*In-room: no a/c (some), no phone (some), kitchen (some), no TV (some). In-hotel: beachfront, water sports, bicycles, laundry service* ⊟*AE, MC, V* ⓧ*EP.*

3

BEACHES

Middle Caicos is blessed with two particularly stunning beaches: Mudjin Harbour and Bamberra Beach. You can hike the trails on the cliffs overlooking Mudjin Harbour and find small private coves. The beach is divided by corals that stick out of the water; on one side the sea is calm, on the other side, the waves crash over the coral. At low tide, sandbars form in the middle. Each summer Bamberra Beach hosts the Middle Caicos Model Sailboat Race. The hand-carved boats are painted in bright colors and can be purchased at the Middle Caicos Coop Shop in Blue Hills in Provo.

SPORTS & THE OUTDOORS

CAVE TOURS

Taxi driver and fisherman **Cardinal Arthur** (☎*649/946–6107*) can give you a good cave tour.

Local cave specialist and taxi driver **Ernest Forbes** (☎*649/946–6140*) can give you a cave tour and may even arrange for you to have a prix-fixe lunch at his house afterward if you ask nicely.

GUIDED TOURS

George Gibbs (☎*649/243–8371*) knows all the crevices in the reefs and will take you lobster hunting: fun during the day followed by a delicious night.

SOUTH CAICOS

This 8½-square-mi (21-square-km) island with a population of only 1,400 was once an important salt producer; today it is the heart of the country's fishing industry. You'll find long, white beaches, jagged bluffs, quiet backwater bays, and salt flats. The island is so basic and rustic that you may feel as if you are stepping back in time to a sleepier world, where you have to stop the car to allow donkeys and cows to cross the street.

You will see construction all over the island, with two resorts under development. As your plane lands, you can't miss the construction site for the Caicos Beach Club Resort & Marina sitting perched on a hill; it has changed developers several times and was first scheduled to open in 2005. Now seven buildings are in various stages of completion (the clubhouse is finished), so some progress is being made. When finished, the resort will be huge, with some 700 rooms, a casino, and a marina. A 200-room resort is being built on East Bay Beach.

In September 2008 Hurricanes Hanna and Ike gave South Caicos a one–two punch, and many of the buildings at Cockburn Harbour sustained substantial damage; island residents had to wait over a month to have power restored. Although the town is still in disarray at this writing, the dive sites are fine, and South Caicos Ocean Beach Resort, the only place to stay on South Caicos, and South Caicos Divers, the main dive outfitter, are both up and running. Also, there are four places to eat (two of them open only occasionally for dinner).

The major draw for South Caicos is its excellent diving and snorkeling on the pristine wall and reefs (with an average visibility of 100 feet). This is a treat enjoyed by only a few, but it's practically the only thing to do on South Caicos other than to lie on the lovely beaches. Several local fishermen harvest spiny lobsters for the Turks and Caicos and for export. Making up the third-largest reef in the world, the coral walls surrounding South Caicos are dramatic, dropping dramatically from 50 feet to 6,000 feet in the blink of an eye.

GETTING THERE

The only way to reach South Caicos is by air on a flight from Provo on Air Turks & Caicos.

Airline Contacts Air Turks & Caicos (☎649/941–5481 ⊕www. airturksandcaicos.com).

EXPLORING SOUTH CAICOS

At the northern end of the island are fine white-sand beaches; the south coast is great for scuba diving along the drop-off; and there's excellent snorkeling off the windward (east) coast, where large stands of elkhorn and staghorn coral shelter several varieties of small tropical fish. Spiny lobster and queen conch are found in the shallow Caicos Bank to the west, and are harvested for export by local processing plants. The bonefishing here is some of the best in the West Indies.

Boiling Hole. Abandoned salinas (natural salt pans) make up the center of this island—the largest, across from the downtown ballpark, receives its water directly from an underground source connected to the ocean through this boiling hole.

Cockburn Harbour. The best natural harbor in the Caicos chain hosts the South Caicos Regatta, held each year in May.

WHERE TO STAY & EAT

Restaurant choices on South Caicos are limited, and no one takes credit cards, so bring cash. Except for the Dolphin Pub at the South Caicos Ocean & Beach Resort, the three best places are operated directly out of the owner's homes. **Love's** restaurant (on Airport Rd.) offers a daily changing menu of fresh seafood priced from $8 to $15. **Darryl's** (on Stubbs Rd.) is another casual restaurant that offers whatever is brought in for the day; expect to pay $10 to $20. Ask around to find out when (or if) these local favorites will be open; neither has a phone.

$$ ✕ **Dolphin Pub.** Located at South Caicos Ocean & Beach Resort, it's the only real restaurant on the island. The food is casual; you'll find burgers, chicken, and fish. There is some Asian influence in the sauces and rice, and there are certainly Caribbean influences in the jerk sauce on the fish. At night this turns into a gathering place for guests who tell their tales about the sea, the fish that they caught, or the sea eagle ray that they spotted while diving. If you are around for lunch (most visitors to South Caicos will be scuba diving), this is your only choice. ✉*Turker Hill* ☎*649/946–3810* ▭*No credit cards.*

$–$$ ✕ **Muriel's.** Muriel serves dinner most nights in her home but has no fixed menu. This is the most reliable of the three home-based businesses on the island, though you must call ahead. Dinner will likely be the catch of the day. ⊠*Graham St., Cockburn Harbour* ☎*649/946–3535* ⚲*Reservations essential* ⊟*No credit cards* ⊙*No lunch.*

$$ ⊡**South Caicos Ocean & Beach Resort.** Rustic and basic—though perfectly acceptable—this is your only lodging option in South Caicos. The two-story building has balconies or patios with views of the never-ending turquoise water. Rooms are spacious and painted in pastels, giving sense of tranquillity; the beds are plush with pillow-top mattresses. It's a nice place to hang out with other divers, who are the primary clientele; the hotel offers dive-stay packages with South Caicos Divers, which is on the property. **Pros:** each room has stunning views of the Caicos Banks; the best scuba diving off South Caicos is in front of the hotel; it has the only real restaurant on the island. **Cons:** you need to bring cash to pay for everything but your room; not on the beach. ⊠*Turker Hill* ☎*649/946–3810* ⊕*www.SouthCaicosOceanBeachResort.com* ↩*24 rooms, 6 apartments* ⚲*In room: refrigerator (some), no TV. In-hotel: restaurant, bar, pool, diving, bicycles, parking (no fee), no-smoking rooms* ⊟*AE, MC, V EP.*

BEACHES

The beaches at **Belle Sound** on South Caicos will take your breath away, with lagoon-like waters. Expect the beach to be natural and rustic—after storms you will see some seaweed. To the north of South Caicos uninhabited **East Caicos** has a beautiful 17-mi (27-km) beach on its north coast. The island was once a cattle range and the site of a major sisal-growing industry. Both places are accessible only by boat. Due south of South Caicos is **Little Ambergris Cay,** an uninhabited cay about 14 mi (23 km) beyond the Fish Cays, with excellent bonefishing on the second-largest sand bar in the world. On the opposite side of the ridge from Belle Sound, **Long Bay** is an endless stretch of beach, but it can be subjected to rough surf; however, on calmer days you'll feel like you're on a deserted island.

A "Tail" of a Dive

In the 1970s, during the height of drug-running days, planes from Colombia landed all the time on South Caicos. One plane, a Convair 29A (the size of a DC-3), ran out of gas as it approached the runway. The pilot survived, but the plane did not. The wings and body stayed intact, the nose and tail broke off as the plane crashed into the ocean. The pieces now sit in about 50 feet of water, and they are almost completely encrusted with coral. The dive site is in two parts: "The Plane" is the main hub with the body and wings; the "Warhead" is the tail of the wreck a few yards away. Usually there are schools of snapper and Jacks swimming through the wreck, and at night, sometimes sharks, making it a unique dive. As you land at the airport, the wreck can be seen from the air.

SPORTS & THE OUTDOORS

DIVING

The reef walls that surround South Caicos are part of the third-largest reef system in the world. The reef starts at about 50 feet and then drops dramatically to around 6,000 feet. Most sights on the walls have no names, but you can dive anywhere along them. The visibility is ideal—consistently more than 100 feet and most times beyond that.

The Caves on Long Cay (which you can see out your window at the South Caicos Ocean & Beach Resort) are really five caves under the water that were made for exploring. **The Maze,** suitable only for expert divers, will keep you swimming at 105 feet through tunnels before you pop out at 75 feet.**The Arch,** so named because it resembles a natural bridge in Aruba (only under the water) offers the opportunity to see both eagle rays and sharks.

The Blue Hole is similar to the Blue Hole in Belize, but this one is under the ocean rather than on land. It's a natural sinkhole in the middle of the ocean between Middle Caicos and South Caicos on the Caicos Banks that drops to 250 feet. From the air, it looks like a dark blue circle in the middle of a turquoise sea.

Sharks, barracuda, octopus, green morays, eagle rays, and lobster are only some of the sea creatures that are common to these waters.During whale-watching season from mid-January to mid-April you can watch adult whales teach their babies how to clean themselves on the sand patches within view of South Caicos Ocean & Beach Resort.

South Caicos Divers(⊠*Turker Hill* ☎*649/331–1800* ⊕*www. SouthCaicosDiver.com*) offers everything you need to enjoy these pristine waters any time of the day or night, from two-tank morning dives to afternoon dives to night dives; it can guide you to both wreck and cave dives. Owner Greg's experience with the waters of South Caicos can't be matched. He also rents equipment that can be used on the reefs in front of the South Caicos Ocean & Beach Resort, next door. The resort teams up with South Caicos Divers to offer dive- and meal-inclusive plans.

FISHING

Beyond the Blue (⊠*Cockburn Town* ☎*649/231–1703* ⊕*www.beyondtheblue.com*) offers bonefishing charters on a specialized airboat, which can operate in less than a foot of water. Lodging packages are available.

AMBERGRIS CAYS

20–25 minutes by air from Provo.

Ambergris Cay has much to offer to the lucky few who visit. It's a small, flat island next to the second-largest sandbar in the world, and it's one of the few places you can go to see untouched fields of the national symbol, the Turks head cactus. Iguanas roam freely, and flamingos fly by. Up until the 1960s whaling, which was banned by international law, was practiced here. Now the focus is on watching the whales from this incredible vantage point.

Privately owned Ambergris Cay is being developed into an upscale destination by the **Turks & Caicos Sporting Club** (*Ambergris Cay* ☎*877/815–1300* ⊕*www.TCSportingClub. com*). At this writing there are seven completed villas on the island, along with housing for the resident staff. A spa, restaurant, and resort amenities are offered.

Adjacent to Ambergris Cay, **Little Ambergris Cay** has some of the best bonefishing in the world; so big are the schools that you can almost tire of reeling them in.

GETTING THERE

Most people reach Ambergris Cay by private plane; however, landing here is an adventure, since the landing strip sticks out over the water.

Grand Turk

WORD OF MOUTH

"We enjoyed the people and the island. Wild donkeys, horses, and cows roam freely."

—Eagle

"We took a day trip to Grand Turk, and it was a neat island. We wouldn't mind spending a few days there to unwind."

—MyMoosie

By
Ramona
Settle

SLEEPY, LAID-BACK, LAZY, AND CHARMING, Grand Turk is the kind of place that you either love or can't wait to leave. Rich in history, the island's historic buildings were made mostly from scraps of the ships of pirates who were tricked into coming ashore. Locals walk slowly down the street in the heat of the sun, wearing big floppy hats or under parasols. Perfectionists and guests who want the latest and trendiest may not appreciate the island's rustic, laid-back charm, but photographers and divers delight in the colors and authentic ambience, and vacationers looking to simply relax will find much to like about Grand Turk.

Just 7 mi (11 km) long and a little over 1 mi (2½ km) wide, this island, with a population of 3,700, is the capital and seat of the Turks and Caicos government. It has been a longtime favorite destination of divers eager to explore the 7,000-foot-deep pristine coral walls that drop down only 300 yards out to sea. On shore, the tiny, quiet island has white-sand beaches, the national museum, and a small population of wild horses and donkeys, which meander past the white-walled courtyards, pretty churches, and bougainvillea-covered colonial inns on their daily commute into town. History here mixes with nature.

Many argue that Grand Turk was the actual first landfall during Christopher Columbus's first voyage to the New World—not the Bahamas, which has always been the traditional location. You will see national park signs making this claim all along Front Street. The island first gained international recognition in 1962, when John Glenn's Mercury spacecraft splashed down nearby after he became the first astronaut to orbit the earth. You can see a replica of his rocket ship outside the airport.

A cruise-ship complex that opened at the southern end of the island in 2006 now brings some 300,000 visitors per year. Despite the dramatic changes this could have made to this peaceful tourist spot, the dock is pretty much self-contained, and is about 3 mi (5 km) from the tranquil, small hotels of Cockburn Town, Pillory Beach, and the Ridge, and far from most of the western-shore dive sites. The influx of tourists has had a mostly positive effect on the island, pushing Grand Turk to open up a few new historic sites, including Grand Turk's old prison and the lighthouse. Otherwise, the atmosphere is pretty much the same.

In September 2008 Grand Turk was devastated by a one–two punch from Hurricanes Hanna and Ike. As luck would have it, the reefs did not suffer any serious damage, and divers were back in the waters in a few days. Electricity was slower to return, but most of the island's hotels had reopened by January 2009.

At this writing the landscape was in full bloom and poised to bounce back as well.

EXPLORING GRAND TURK

Circling the island is easy, since it's only 7 mi long and 1 mi wide. On a day trip you can have fun for a couple of hours and still have time to relax in the sun the same afternoon. Stroll down Front Street with its historic buildings, making sure to stop in the excellent museum. If there is a cruise ship in port, check out the old prison and go to the lighthouse. Dive the crystal-clear waters or feed the stingrays at Gibb's Cay. People-watch and do some light shopping at the cruise port. End the day at the Sand Bar with tales of your adventures. Those with more time will be able to relax and see the island's sights and enjoy its beautiful beaches and dive sites at their leisure.

ABOUT THE HOTELS
Don't come to Grand Turk expecting five-star resorts with full service and amenities. The first tourists on the island were divers who didn't require much from lodgings. Most accommodations are bed-and-breakfasts or small, humble homes. Some are in historic mansions, and there are a few small hotels. All are clean and comfortable, and offer all the updates you have come to expect when traveling. Changes are on the way: a megachain, Wyndham, is developing a property here—we hope it won't change the personality of the island.

ABOUT THE RESTAURANTS
The restaurants here are small and charming, used as gathering places. Most are set either in courtyards under huge trees and flowering bushes, or next to the beach with sweeping views. Most places are associated with hotels or other lodgings. The chefs know how to turn the fresh catch into fine dining; the ambience is laid-back and relaxing. At the end of the day most restaurants turn into nightlife venues, where people gather to talk of their underwater sightings.

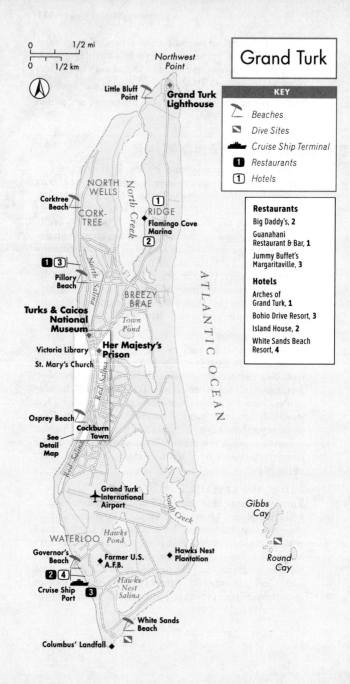

Grand Turk

KEY

⚓ Beaches

◣ Dive Sites

⛴ Cruise Ship Terminal

1 Restaurants

① Hotels

Restaurants

Big Daddy's, **2**

Guanahani
Restaurant & Bar, **1**

Jummy Buffet's
Margaritaville, **3**

Hotels

Arches of
Grand Turk, **1**

Bohio Drive Resort, **3**

Island House, **2**

White Sands Beach
Resort, **4**

0   1/2 mi
0   1/2 km

Northwest Point

Little Bluff Point

Grand Turk Lighthouse

NORTH WELLS

North Creek

CORKTREE

Corktree Beach

① RIDGE

Flamingo Cove Marina

2

North Salina

1 **3**

Pillory Beach

BREEZY BRAE

Town Pond

Turks & Caicos National Museum

Victoria Library

St. Mary's Church

Her Majesty's Prison

ATLANTIC OCEAN

Red Salina

Osprey Beach

See Detail Map

Cockburn Town

Red Salina

Grand Turk International Airport

South Creek

WATERLOO

Hawks Pond

Governor's Beach

Former U.S. A.F.B.

Hawks Nest Plantation

2 **4**

Hawks Nest Salina

⛴

Cruise Ship Port

3

Gibbs Cay

◣

Round Cay

White Sands Beach

Columbus' Landfall

WHAT IT COSTS IN U.S. DOLLARS				
¢	$	$$	$$$	$$$$
RESTAURANTS				
under $8	$8–$12	$12–$20	$20–$30	over $30
HOTELS*				
under $80	$80–$150	$150–$250	$250–$350	over $350
HOTELS**				
under $125	$125–$250	$250–$350	$350–$450	over $450

*EP, BP, CP **AI, FAP, MAP
Restaurant prices are for a main course at dinner and include any taxes or service charges. Hotel prices are per night for a double room in high season, excluding taxes, service charges, and meal plans (except at all-inclusives).

GETTING THERE

Unless you are arriving on a cruise ship, you'll need to fly to Grand Turk from Provo on Air Turks & Caicos, which currently has the only scheduled flights there. Spirit's flights to the island from Fort Lauderdale have been discontinued.

Contacts Air Turks & Caicos (☎649/941–5481 ⊕www.airturksandcaicos.com).

GETTING AROUND

If you are staying anywhere on Duke Street or Front Street, you can easily walk to some of the beaches, to excursion companies, and to the best restaurants. You'll need a car if you want to explore beyond town, but Grand Turk is small, and a self-guided island tour takes just a few hours. You need transportation to reach the lighthouse or Grand Turk Cruise Terminal.

If you want a rental car or want to hire a taxi to get around, check out **Tony's Taxi and Rental Cars** (✉Airport ☎649/946–1979 ⊕www.tonyscarrental.com). He's based at the airport, or you can have him pick you up at any of the island's hotels. You can rent a car from him and explore on your own, or you can hire him to give you a guided tour.

TOP REASONS TO GO

History. Take a morning flight from Provo to Grand Turk and find out how such a small island can have so much history. Travel to the lighthouse, visit the old prison where the last hanging was as recent as 1960, and certainly visit the national museum; you'll be smarter by the time you hit the beach to relax in the afternoon.

Dive the Wall. The coral walls drop off to thousands of feet as little as 300 feet offshore in Grand Turk—it's even possible to swim to the wall from the beach. The less time it takes to reach the site, the more time to enjoy your dive.

Old Caribbean Charm. In Grand Turk you'll feel like you've stepped back in time. Giving meaning to "island time," locals just take it slow. On Front Street layers of sun-bleached, peeling paint only add to the charm. Walk down the street and everyone smiles and says hello; some will even stop to converse and are truly interested in where you're from. Watch where you walk; you'll share the road with wild donkeys and roosters.

Shopping and Playing at the Cruise Port. So you think you can't mix Old Caribbean charm with a 3,000-passenger cruise ship? The beauty of Grand Turk is that despite its small size, these two happily coexist, and fickle vacationers can have it both ways: the relaxation of a slower life, and just 3 mi away, the bustle of shops and pool games. But the bustle is only bustling (and available) when there is a cruise ship at the dock.

Gibbs Cay. A 20-minute boat ride from Front Street takes you along the shore to an uninhabited cay for snorkeling; in another five minutes you're in Gibbs Cay. The stingrays already sense the boat coming, and they will swim with you the whole time you are there. It's a don't-miss experience.

WHAT TO SEE

Pristine beaches with vistas of turquoise waters, small local settlements, historic ruins, and native flora and fauna are among the sights on Grand Turk. About 3,700 people live on this 7½-square-mi (19-square-km) island, and it's hard to get lost, as there aren't many roads.

Cockburn Town. The buildings in the colony's capital and seat of government reflect a 19th-century Bermudian style. Narrow streets are lined with low stone walls and old street lamps, which are now powered by electricity. The once-vital salinas (natural salt pans, where the sea leaves a film of salt) have been restored, and covered benches along the sluices offer shady spots for observing wading birds, including flamingos that frequent the shallows. Be sure to pick up a copy of the tourist board's Heritage Walk guide to discover Grand Turk's rich architecture.

Her Majesty's Prison (⊠*Pond St., Cockburn Town* ☎*No phone*☜*Free* ☉ *Open only when a cruise ship is docked*) was built in the 19th century to house runaway slaves and slaves who survived the wreck of the *Trouvadore* in 1841. After the slaves were granted freedom, the prison housed criminals and even modern-day drug runners until it closed in the 1990s. The last hanging here was in 1960. Now you can see the cells, solitary confinement area, and exercise patio. The prison is only open when there is a cruise ship at the port.

⟲ In one of the oldest stone buildings on the islands, the **Turks**
★ **& Caicos National Museum** houses the Molasses Reef wreck, the earliest shipwreck—dating from the early 1500s—discovered in the Americas. The natural-history exhibits include artifacts left by Taíno, African, North American, Bermudian, French, and Latin American settlers. The museum has a 3-D coral reef exhibit, a walk-in Lucayan cave with wooden artifacts, and a gallery dedicated to Grand Turk's little-known involvement in the Space Race (John Glenn made landfall here after being the first American to orbit the Earth). An interactive children's gallery keeps knee-high visitors "edutained." The museum also claims that Grand Turk was where Columbus first landed in the New World. The most original display is a collection of messages in bottles that have washed ashore from all over the world. ⊠*Duke St., Cockburn Town* ☎*649/946–2160* ⊕*www.tcmuseum.org* ☜*$5* ☉*Mon., Tues., Thurs., and Fri. 9–4; Wed. 9–5; Sat. 9–1.*

Grand Turk Lighthouse. More than 150 years old, the lighthouse, built in the United Kingdom and transported piece by piece to the island, used to protect ships in danger of wrecking on the northern reefs. Use this panoramic landmark as a starting point for a breezy cliff-top walk by following the donkey trails to the deserted eastern beach. ⊠*Lighthouse Rd., North Ridge.*

WHERE TO EAT

Conch in every shape and form, fresh grouper, and lobster (in season) are the favorite dishes at the laid-back restaurants that line Duke Street. Away from these more touristy areas, smaller and less expensive eateries serve chicken and ribs, curried goat, peas and rice, and other native island specialties. Prices are more expensive than in the United States, as most of the produce has to be imported.

COCKBURN TOWN

$$–$$$ ✕**Birdcage Restaurant.** At the top of Duke Street, this has
★ become the place to be on Sunday and Wednesday nights, when a sizzling barbecue of ribs, chicken, and lobster combines with live "rake-and-scrape" music from a local group called High Tide to draw an appreciative crowd. Arrive before 8 PM to secure beachside tables and an unrestricted view of the band; the location around the Osprey pool is lovely. The rest of the week, enjoy more elegant and eclectic fare accompanied by an increasingly impressive wine list. ⊠*Osprey Beach Hotel, Duke St., Cockburn Town* ☎*649/946–2666* ⊟*MC, V.*

$ ✕**Mookie Pookie Pizza Palace.** Local husband-and-wife team "Mookie" and "Pookie" have created a wonderful back-street parlor that has gained well-deserved popularity over the years as much more than a pizza place. At lunchtime the tiny eatery is packed with locals ordering specials like steamed beef, curried chicken, and curried goat. You can also get burgers and omelets, but stick to the specials if you want fast service, and dine in if you want to get a true taste of island living. By night the place becomes Grand Turk's one and only pizza take-out and delivery service, so if you're renting a villa or condo, put this spot on speed dial. ⊠*Hospital Rd., Cockburn Town* ☎*649/946–1538* ⊟*No credit cards* ☉*Closed Sun.*

✕**Sand Bar.** Run by two Canadian sisters, this popular beachside bar is a good value, though the menu is limited to fish-and-chips, quesadillas, and similarly basic bar fare. The tented wooden terrace jutting out onto the beach provides shade during the day, making it an ideal lunch spot, but it's also a great place to watch the sunset. The service is friendly, and the local crowd often spills into the street. ⊠*Duke St., Cockburn Town* ☎*No phone* ⊟*MC, V.*

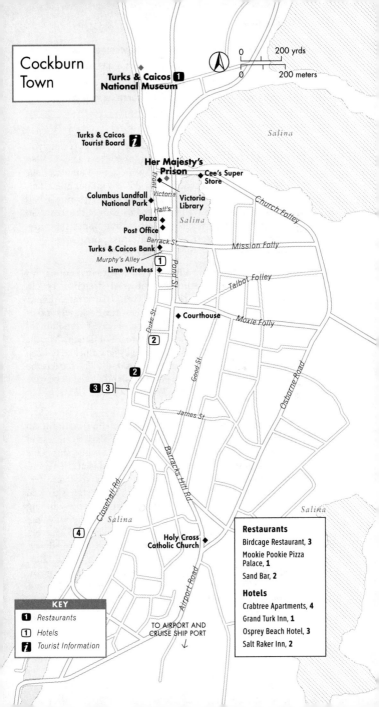

Cockburn Town

Turks & Caicos 1
National Museum

Turks & Caicos
Tourist Board 𝒊

Her Majesty's
Prison

Columbus Landfall
National Park

Plaza

Post Office

Turks & Caicos Bank

Murphy's Alley — 1

Lime Wireless

Cee's Super
Store

Victoria
Library

Victoria

Hall's

Salina

Barrack St.

Pond St.

Front St.

Salina

Church Folley

Mission Folly

Talbot Folley

Moxie Folly

1

2

2

3 3

Duke St.

Good St.

Courthouse

James St.

Osborne Road

4

Closehall Rd.

Barracks Hill Rd.

Salina

Holy Cross
Catholic Church

Salina

Airport Road

TO AIRPORT AND
CRUISE SHIP PORT
↓

0   200 yrds
0   200 meters

Restaurants
Birdcage Restaurant, 3
Mookie Pookie Pizza
Palace, 1
Sand Bar, 2

Hotels
Crabtree Apartments, 4
Grand Turk Inn, 1
Osprey Beach Hotel, 3
Salt Raker Inn, 2

KEY
1 *Restaurants*
1 *Hotels*
𝒊 *Tourist Information*

GRAND TURK LIVE. Want to know what the weather is like on Grand Turk? Now you can check it 24 hours a day at the Web site ⊕www.grandturkcc.com, the Web site for the Grand Turk Cruise Center. You can also check to see if there's a ship in port.

ELSEWHERE ON GRAND TURK

$–$$ ✕**Big Daddy's.** A location next to the cruise port puts you close to the hub but far enough away to relax. Grilled sandwiches with tropical coleslaw are served under a huge gazebo facing the beach. The food is casual but great. Service can be slow, but in a place like this it's not a bad thing—you'll just have more time to admire the view. Go on karaoke night, when you get to sing under the stars. ⊠ *White Sands Resort, next to the cruise port, Grand Turk Cruise Terminal* ☎*649/946–2991* ▭*MC, V.*

✕**Guanahani Restaurant & Bar.** Off the town's main drag, this restaurant sits on a stunning but quiet stretch of beach. The food goes beyond the usual Grand Turk fare, thanks to the talents of Canadian-born chef Zev Beck, who takes care of the evening meals. His pecan-encrusted mahimahi and crispy sushi rolls are to die for. For lunch, Middle Caicos native Miss Leotha makes juicy jerk chicken to keep the crowd happy. The menu changes daily. The food is the best in Grand Turk, but it's also the island's most expensive restaurant. ⊠*Bohio Dive Resort & Spa, Pillory Beach* ☎*649/946–2135* ▭*MC, V.*

$$ ✕**Jimmy Buffet's Margaritaville.** The only chain restaurant (so far) in all of the Turks and Caicos is the place to engage in cruise activities even when you're not on a cruise ship. One of the largest Margaritavilles in the world is at the Grand Turk Cruise Terminal and open to all comers (both cruisers and anyone else on the island) when a cruise ship is parked at the dock. Tables are scattered around a large winding pool; there's even a DJ and a FlowRider (a wave pool where you can surf on land—for a fee). You can enjoy 52 flavors of margaritas or the restaurant's own beer, Landshark, while you eat casual bar food such as wings, quesadillas, and burgers. The food is good, the people-watching is great. ⊠ *Grand Turk Cruise Terminal* ☎*649/946–1880* ⊕ *www.margaritavillecaribbean.com* ▭*AE, D, DC, MC, V* ⊘*Closed when no cruise ships is at the pier.*

WHERE TO STAY

Accommodations include original Bermudian inns, more modern but small beachfront hotels, and very basic to well-equipped self-catering suites and apartments. Almost all hotels offer dive packages, which are an excellent value.

COCKBURN TOWN

$$ ⊞**Crabtree Apartments.** On their own secluded stretch of beach, these three apartments make a quiet getaway that is far enough from the cruise-ship port to give you some peace and quiet, but still within walking distance of Duke and Front streets. The apartments are decorated with wicker and colorful Haitian paintings; there are overstuffed chairs on the covered patio. The apartments are right on the beach, which has its own secluded cove, so you'll definitely feel out of the fray. Grand Turk is quiet and laid-back, with plenty of Old Caribbean charm, just like this complex. **Pros:** private beachfront; the art on the walls adds a tropical touch. **Cons:** hard to find; a longer walk to restaurants than from hotels closer to town; five-night minimum makes it hard to use as a base for a quick trip from Provo. ⊠ *Close Hall Rd., Cockburn Town* ☎649/468–2410 ⊕*www.Grand Turk VacationRental.com* ⊅3 2-bedroom apartments ⌕In-room: kitchen. In-hotel: beachfront, bicycles, laundry facilities, parking (no fee), no-smoking rooms ⊟MC, V ⌕5 night min. ⊺⊚|EP.

$$$ ⊞**Grand Turk Inn Bed & Breakfast.** With a prime location on Front Street in Grand Turk, this is a true B&B, one of just a few in all the Turks and Caicos islands. Staying here gives you a feel for the way the Caribbean used to be, without requiring you to give up comfort. Sleepy, quiet, and charming, it does feel like a home away from home, but with a better view. The home is updated with all the modern conveniences, including air-conditioning, satellite TV, and luxury colonial-style furnishings; each suite has a full kitchen with two TVs and a DVD player. A huge sundeck on the rooftop faces the stunning water. You can easily stroll back and forth to Front Street, with its excellent restaurants and watering holes, to listen to musicians play and to hear (and tell) tall tales. Staying here, you will certainly meet and mingle with the locals, so when you return, you'll feel as if you are returning home, just as other guests do who return year after year. **Pros:** charming old Caribbean clapboard house; faces the beach; all guests lent a

CLOSE UP

Of Hurricanes & Wild Weather

Since 1984, when the increase in tourism began here, the Turks and Caicos have largely escaped the wrath of hurricanes and tropical storms that have battered the nearby Bahamas regularly. As one of the driest island chains in the southern Atlantic, they rarely even get much rainfall.

Even during a rare and much-needed downpour, you may see rain on one part of Provo but not a drop on the other side of the island. When a weather report says there is a 30% to 60% chance of rain, you can usually assume that only *one* of the islands in the archipelago might get a rain shower but not the others. There could be rain on North Caicos, for example, but not even a cloud in the skies over Provo. Sometimes you will see rain even as the sun is shining on you! These sun showers only last a couple of minutes. An hour of rain is often followed by an hour of bright sunlight.

A major hurricane had not hit the Turks and Caicos directly for over 50 years. But in September 2008 the islands received a double whammy: back-to-back hurricanes—Hurricane Hanna and Hurricane Ike—and just a week apart. During Hanna, a Category 1 storm, the hurricane's eye passed over Provo an unusual three times; the storm then remained stationary over the island for almost four full days, dumping water 24 hours a day. No one had prepared for Hanna, since forecasts had not shown it passing anywhere close to Provo.

Less than a week later Hurricane Ike—a Category 4 storm—passed through the island chain. Most buildings on Provo lost roof shingles and basic landscaping, but the island bounced back fairly quickly.

On Grand Turk, Salt Cay, and South Caicos it was a different story entirely. There was so much destruction and disarray that it took months just to restore power to the islands. Construction companies from Provo sent workers over quickly to help restore the harder-hit islands, and the cruise lines that call in Grand Turk also sent help. In fact, the cruise stops resumed about a month later, on October 8, 2008.

The surrounding reefs are all in fine shape and sustained no damage. At this writing not everything is up and running on Grand Turk and Salt Cay yet, so double-check before making your travel plans. If you are traveling during hurricane season, it's always wise to get travel insurance, even if a major hurricane strike takes another 50 years.

local cell phone. **Cons:** no kids under 16. ✉*Front St., Cockburn Town* 🕾*649/946–2827* ⊕ *www.GrandTurkInn.com* 🛏*5 rooms* ⌂*In-hotel: safe, DVD, Wi-Fi. In-hotel: beachfront, bicycles, laundry facilities, laundry service, Wi-Fi, parking (free), no kids under 16, no-smoking rooms* ☰*AE, DC, MC, V BP.*

★ **Fodor's**Choice🏨**Osprey Beach Hotel.** Grand Turk veteran hotelier
$–$$ Jenny Smith has transformed this two-story oceanfront hotel with her artistic touches. Palms, frangipani, and deep green azaleas frame it like a painting. Inside, evocative island watercolors, painted by her longtime friend, Nashville artist Tupper Saussay, are featured throughout the property. Vaulted ceilings and Indonesian four-poster beds are the highlight of upstairs Suites 51, 52, and 53. Downstairs you can enjoy beach access through your own garden. On the opposite side of Duke Street the newly built suites have phones, TVs, and Wi-Fi service. **Pros:** renovated in 2007; best hotel on Grand Turk; walking distance to Front Street, restaurants, and excursions. **Cons:** three-night minimum; rocky beachfront. ✉*Duke St., Cockburn Town* 🕾*649/946–2666* ⊕*www.ospreybeachhotel.com* 🛏*11 rooms, 16 suites* ⌂*In-room: Wi-Fi (some), kitchen (some). In-hotel: restaurant, bar, pool, beachfront, water sports, laundry service, some pets allowed* ☰*AE, MC, V* ☞*3-night min.* ❑*EP.*

$–$$ 🏨**Salt Raker Inn.** A large anchor on the sun-dappled pathway marks the entrance to this 19th-century house, which is now an unpretentious inn. The building was built by a shipwright, and has a large, breezy balcony with commanding views over the sea, but its best feature is hidden behind the facade: a secret garden of tall tamarind and neme trees, climbing vines, hanging plants, potted hibiscus, climbing bougainvillea, and even a pond. The greenery, as well as providing a quiet spot for natural shade, is home to the inn's Secret Garden Restaurant. Rooms A2, B2, and C2 are nicely shaded havens but have no sea views. Upstairs, Rooms G and H share a balcony with unobstructed views of the ocean and Duke Street. At this writing, damage from Hurricane Ike in 2008 was still being repaired, but the inn was still open during construction. The inn and restaurant were expected to open fully by late summer 2009. **Pros:** excellent location that is an easy walk to Front Street, restaurants, and excursions. **Cons:** no no-smoking rooms. ✉*Duke St., Box 1, Cockburn Town* 🕾*649/946–2260* ⊕*www.hotelsaltraker.com* 🛏*10 rooms, 3 suites* ⌂*In-room:*

4

refrigerator, Wi-Fi. In-hotel: restaurant, bar, laundry service, some pets allowed, Wi-Fi ⊟D, MC, V ⦁⊙⦁EP.

ELSEWHERE ON GRAND TURK

$$ ⬚**Arches of Grand Turk.** Upstairs and downstairs, east- and west-facing balconies from these four ridge-top town houses ensure nicely framed views of both sunrise and sunset. Canadian husband-and-wife team Wally and Cecile Wennick left Florida in the 1990s after more than a decade in the hospitality industry to create this hillside home away from home, less than a five-minute walk from the deserted east beach. The well-equipped town houses are peppered with Cecile's handicrafts, including painted glass bottles, embroidery, and wall hangings that combine to give the airy houses a homespun feel. Weekly housekeeping is included in the rate, but daily maid service costs extra. **Pros:** quiet getaway; feels like home. **Cons:** not on the beach; requires a car. ⊠*Lighthouse Rd., Box 226* ☎649/946–2941 ⊕*www. grandturkarches.com* ⤴*4 town houses* ⅄*In-room: kitchen, Wi-Fi. In-hotel: pool, bicycles, laundry service, Wi-Fi, Internet terminal* ⊟D, MC, V ⦁⊙⦁EP.

$$ ⬚**Bohio Dive Resort & Spa.** Formerly the Pillory Beach Resort, this small hotel sits on an otherwise deserted stretch of beach. It's a dream come true for British couple Kelly Shanahan and Nick Gillings, who have created their own retreat on Grand Turk after years of visiting the tiny island. The resort's restaurant is the best on the island. You can relax with yoga sessions or party with the locals at the Sunday sail and kayak races or Thursday-night's "pit party" with roasted meats and music. **Pros:** has the best restaurant in Grand Turk; on a gorgeous beach; steps away from awesome snorkeling. **Cons:** rooms are basic and dated; three-night minimum. ⊠*Pillory Beach* ☎649/946–2135 ⊕*www. bohioresort.com* ⤴*12 rooms, 4 suites* ⅄*In-room: kitchen (some), no phone. In-hotel: restaurant, bars, pool, spa, beachfront, diving, water sports, Internet terminal* ⊟AE, MC, V ⤳*3-night min.* ⦁⊙⦁EP.

$$ ⬚**Island House.** Owner Colin Brooker gives his guests a
☽ personal introduction to the capital island, thanks to his family's long history here. Years of business-travel experience have helped Colin create the comfortable, peaceful suites that overlook North Creek. Balcony barbecues, shaded hammocks, and flat-screen TVs are among the

diversions from the backdrop of splendid island and ocean views. Suites 3 and 7 command the best sunset views. Graduated terraces descend the hillside to a small pool surrounded by pink-and-white climbing bougainvillea, creating the feel of a Mediterranean hideaway. An array of inflatable toys keeps kids happy. The deserted east beach is a 12-minute walk away. If you stay more than three nights, a car is included in the rental price. **Pros:** full condo units feel like a home away from home. **Cons:** not on the beach; you need a car to get around. ⊠*Lighthouse Rd., Box 36* ☎*649/946–1519* ⊕*www.islandhouse-tci.com* ⇨*8 suites* ☌*In-room: kitchen, Wi-Fi. In-hotel: pool, water sports, bicycles, laundry facilities, Wi-Fi, some pets allowed* ☐*AE, D, MC, V* ⎮○⎮*EP.*

$\$$ ⌂**White Sands Beach Resort.** These condos offer a glimpse into two separate worlds: though the location puts you next to the cruise-ship port with its daily action, you're still on a quiet stretch of beach just made for relaxing. All the units are identical, fully furnished one-bedroom apartments with full kitchens, a living and dining area, and direct views of the beach and ocean. A small pool is on the property, but you can also walk next door to use the huge pool at Margaritaville in the cruise-ship port. The restaurant, Big Daddy's, has the best casual food on the island. You need a car or bicycle to get around to Front Street, but excursion companies will pick you up on the beachfront. A huge gazebo on the beach is the perfect place to watch the sunset or try to catch a glimpse of the elusive green flash. **Pros:** situated on a beautiful stretch of beach; gazebo is great for watching the sunset; resort will help set up dive packages with local operators. **Cons:** far enough from the main hub that you need a car or taxi. ⊠*Grand Turk Cruise Terminal* ☎*649/946–1065* ⊕*www. WhiteSandsBeach ResortTCI.com* ⇨*16 apartments* ☌*In room: kitchen, DVD, Wi-Fi. In hotel: restaurant, bar, pool, beachfront, water sports, laundry service, Wi-Fi, parking (free)* ☐*AE, D, DC, MC, V* ⎮○⎮*EP.*

BEACHES

Visitors to Grand Turk will be spoiled when it comes to beach options: sunset strolls along miles of deserted beaches, picnics in secluded coves, beachcombing on the coralline sands, snorkeling around shallow coral heads close to shore, and admiring the impossibly turquoise-blue waters. There are small cove beaches in front of Crabtree Apartments and the Osprey Beach Hotel that you will have pretty much to yourself. The best of the small beaches is next to the Sand Dollar Bar and in front of Oasis Dive Shop; it's also an excellent place for snorkeling right off the beach. The long stretch starting at the Grand Turk Cruise Terminal Beach, followed by White Sands Beach, and ending at Governor's Beach allows miles of walking and beachcombing.

Governor's Beach, a beautiful crescent of powder-soft sand and shallow, calm turquoise waters that fronts the official British Governor's residence, called Waterloo, is framed by tall casuarina trees that provide plenty of natural shade. To have it all to yourself, go on a day when cruise ships are not in port. On days when ships are in port, the beach is lined with lounge chairs.

For a beachcombing experience, **Little Bluff Point Beach,** just west of the Grand Turk Lighthouse, is a low, limestone-cliff-edged, shell-covered beach that looks out onto shallow waters, mangroves, and often flamingos, especially in spring and summer.

★ **Pillory Beach,** with sparkling neon-turquoise water, is the prettiest beach on Grand Turk; it also has great off-the-beach-snorkeling.

White Sands Beach, between the Grand Turk Cruise Terminal and Governor's Beach, has sparkling water that offers more seclusion from the cruise crowds yet access to the terminal and shops (open only when a ship is in port). Old weathered fishing boats parked on the beach offer a contrast with a big shiny cruise ships parked behind them.

SPORTS & THE OUTDOORS

ADVENTURE TOURS

Chukka Caribbean Adventures (⊠*Grand Turk Cruise Terminal* ☎*649/232–1339* ⊕*www.ChukkaCaribbean.com*), the Jamaica-based adventure-tour operator, runs most of the cruise excursions on Grand Turk, but you don't have to be on a cruise ship to take part in the fun. Even if you are staying at a hotel on Grand Turk, you can still sign up for extra activities, though they are only available when a cruise ship is moored at the Grand Turk Cruise Terminal. You can join a group horseback ride and swim, dune-buggy

Cruise Activities for Island Visitors

Grand Turk is a unique destination in that there are places on the island that are only open when there is a cruise ship at the port; the good news is that you don't need to be on a cruise to enjoy most of these sights and activities.

For visitors to Grand Turk, the trick is to visit these places as soon as a ship pulls up but before the passengers have a chance to disembark; since disembarkation on a large ship can take a half-hour or more under the best circumstances, you'll have plenty of time to enjoy some of these sights when

they first open but before the cruise crowds arrive. The lighthouse and the old prison are two possibilities.

The shops at the cruise port are only open when there is a ship in port, and vendors will line Front Street when a ship arrives, so go then if you want to shop.

Some other activities are only offered on cruise days, including ATV tours and guided, off-road dirt-bike rides. So if you happen to be on Grand Turk on a cruise-ship day, take full advantage of everything it has to offer.

safari, or 4x4 safari. In fact, staying on land may offer you an advantage. If you're staying more than a couple of days on the island, you can enjoy them all and not have to limit yourself because of ship time constraints. The only downside is that you have to get yourself to the cruise center. Be sure to call ahead for availability.

CYCLING

The island's mostly flat terrain isn't very taxing, and most roads have hard surfaces. Take water with you: there are few places to stop for refreshments. Most hotels have bicycles available, but you can also rent them for $10 to $15 a day from **Oasis Divers** (⊠*Duke St., Cockburn Town* ☎*649/946–1128* ⊕*www.oasisdivers.com*).

DIVING & SNORKELING

In these waters you can find undersea cathedrals, coral gardens, and countless tunnels, but note that you must carry and present a valid certificate card before you'll be allowed to dive. As its name suggests, the **Black Forest** offers staggering black-coral formations as well as the occasional blacktip shark. In the **Library** you can study fish galore, including large numbers of yellowtail snapper. At the Columbus Passage separating South Caicos from Grand Turk, each side of a 22-mi-wide (35-km-wide) channel drops more than 7,000 feet. From January through March thousands of Atlantic humpback whales swim through en route to their winter breeding grounds. **Gibb's Cay,** a small cay a couple of miles off Grand Turk, makes a great excursion for swimming with stingrays.

Dive outfitters can all be found in Cockburn Town. Two-tank boat dives generally cost $60 to $80. **Blue Water Divers** (⊠*Duke St., Cockburn Town* ☎*649/946–2432* ⊕*www. grandturkscuba.com*) has been in operation on Grand Turk since 1983, and is the only PADI Gold Palm five-star dive center on the island. Owner Mitch will undoubtedly put some of your underwater adventures to music in the evenings, when he plays at the Osprey Beach Hotel or Salt Raker Inn.

Oasis Divers (⊠*Duke St., Cockburn Town* ☎*649/946–1128* ⊕*www.oasisdivers.com*) specializes in complete gear handling and pampering treatment. It also supplies Nitrox and rebreathers.

Besides daily dive trips to the wall, **Sea Eye Diving** (⊠*Duke St., Cockburn Town* ☎*649/946–1407* ⊕*www.seaeyediving. com*) offers encounters with friendly stingrays on a popular snorkeling trip to nearby Gibbs Cay.

SHOPPING

Shopping in Grand Turk is hard to come by—choices are slim. Let's just say that no true shopaholic would want to come here for vacation. You can get the usual T-shirts and dive trinkets at all the dive shops, but there are only a few options for more interesting shopping opportunities. When a ship is in port, the shops at the pier will be open, and these increase your options dramatically. **Grand Turk Inn** (⊠*Front St., Cockburn Town* ☎*649/231–7023*) sells beautiful place mats and clothing with tropical prints.

The Goldsmith (⊠ *Grand Turk Cruise Terminal* ☎*No phone*) has the island's largest selection of jewelry, as well as everything from clothing to cigars. Typical T-shirts and jackets from **Piranha Joe's** (⊠*Grand Turk Cruise Terminal* ☎*No phone*) all have GRAND TURK printed on them. The **Ron Jon Surf Shop** (⊠*Grand Turk Cruise Terminal* ☎*No phone* ⊕*www.*

RonJons.com) sells bathing suits, T-shirts, bumper stickers, and beer mugs with its famous logo on them.

NIGHTLIFE

Grand Turk is a quiet place, where you come to relax and unwind, so most of the nightlife consists of little more than a happy hour at sunset so you have a chance to glimpse the elusive green flash. Most restaurants turn into gathering places where you can talk with the new friends you have made that day, but there a few more nightlife-oriented places that will keep you busy after dark.

Big Daddy's (⊠*White Sands Beach Resort, Cruise Port* ☎*649/946–1038*) has karaoke at night where you sing under the stars. On some evenings you'll be able to catch Mitch Rollings of Blue Water Divers; he often headlines the entertainment at the island's different restaurants.

On weekends and holidays the younger crowd heads over to the **Nookie Hill Club** (⊠*Nookie Hill* ☎*No phone*) for late-night drinking and dancing.

Every Wednesday and Sunday there's lively "rake-and-scrape" music at the **Osprey Beach Hotel** (⊠*Duke St., Cockburn Town* ☎*649/946–2666*).

On Friday, rake-and-scrape bands play at the **Salt Raker Inn** (⊠*Duke St., Cockburn Town* ☎*649/946–2260*).

RAKE-AND-SCRAPE. The official music of Turks and Caicos is call rake-and-scrape (or often "rake 'n' scrape"); it's sometimes also known as ripsaw music. It's reputed to have started on tiny Cat Island in the Bahamas. The music is made using goombay drums, carved out of steel-container drums used during shipping. Other "instruments" are added using tools, especially a carpenter's saw, or whatever is on hand. Its inspiration is the music of Africa, and it is particularly popular on more isolated islands. You can still find rake-and-scrape bands around the islands, but they are more prevalent on Grand Turk and South Caicos.

Salt Cay

WORD OF MOUTH

"[From Provo,] you could day trip to Salt Cay (flight required...). If you are traveling between [January] and April, [this] is one of the best places in the world for whale watching. Sometimes they get so close you can snorkel/swim with them! That's an adventure! "

—blamona

By
Ramona
Settle

IN THE 19TH CENTURY THE SALINAS OF SALT CAY produced much of the world's supply of salt. More than 1,000 people lived on the island then, most employed in the salt industry, at a time when salt was as valuable as gold. When the salt dried up, nearly everyone moved on to other islands. Today, there are only 63 inhabitants. Chances are you will meet quite a few by the end of your stay, whether you're here for one day or many.

As you approach Salt Cay, either by boat or by plane, you may wonder what you've gotten yourself into. The land is dry and brown, the island seems too small to occupy you for even a day trip. Don't worry. Salt Cay has a way of getting into your blood and leaving a lasting impression. By the end of your first day you may very well be plotting a return trip.

There are big plans for Salt Cay, which will change the small island forever, though probably not for several years. Gone will be the donkeys and chickens roaming the streets; in their place will be a luxurious resort and new golf course. If you want to see how the Caribbean was when it was laid-back, sleepy, and colorful, visit the island now before it changes.

EXPLORING SALT CAY

Salt sheds and salinas are silent reminders of the days when the island was a leading producer of salt. Now the salt ponds attract abundant birdlife. Island tours are often conducted by motorized golf cart. From January through April, humpback whales pass by on the way to their winter breeding grounds.

ABOUT THE HOTELS

The accommodations in Salt Cay are basic, with just enough to keep you comfortable. You'll find private villas, apartments, and a couple of small guesthouse-style accommodations. Most visitors who come to Salt Cay won't mind a little rusticity; the island attracts that type of traveler. Come here to enjoy the Caribbean of yesteryear and to enjoy nature. You won't be roughing it—while most places count on sea breezes for cooling, you'll still find the occasional air-conditioner, as well as satellite TV and Wi-Fi. What you do get in every one of our recommended lodgings are pleasant hosts who welcome you like family.

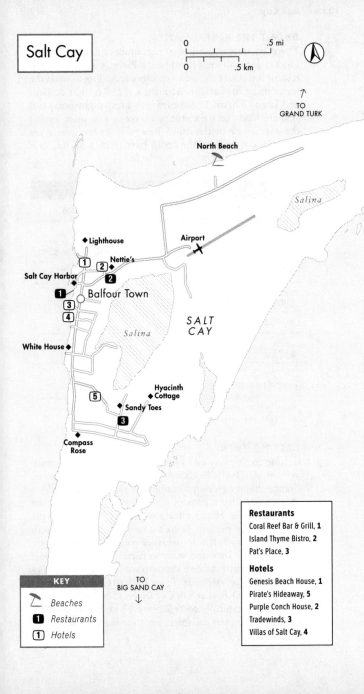

Salt Cay

0   .5 mi

0   .5 km

TO
GRAND TURK

North Beach

Salina

◆ Lighthouse

Airport

1

2 ◆ Nettie's

◆ Salt Cay Harbor

2

1

◯ Balfour Town

3

4

Salina

SALT
CAY

◆ White House

Hyacinth
◆ Cottage

5

◆ Sandy Toes

3

◆ Compass
Rose

TO
BIG SAND CAY
↓

KEY

🏖 *Beaches*

1 *Restaurants*

1 *Hotels*

Restaurants

Coral Reef Bar & Grill, **1**
Island Thyme Bistro, **2**
Pat's Place, **3**

Hotels

Genesis Beach House, **1**
Pirate's Hideaway, **5**
Purple Conch House, **2**
Tradewinds, **3**
Villas of Salt Cay, **4**

ABOUT THE RESTAURANTS

There are only a handful of restaurants on Salt Cay, but food is generally excellent. Pat's Place is a home-based restaurant, where the menu changes according to what the boats bring in that day. At night Coral Reef Bar & Grill and Island Thyme Bistro turn into lively nightspots, and you are likely to see virtually everyone you meet during the day at one or the other. Reservations for dinner are essential everywhere; the cooks have to plan ahead, so if you just show up you may not be fed.

WHAT IT COSTS IN U.S. DOLLARS				
¢	$	$$	$$$	$$$$
RESTAURANTS				
under $8	$8–$12	$12–$20	$20–$30	over $30
HOTELS*				
under $80	$80–$150	$150–$250	$250–$350	over $350
HOTELS**				
under $125	$125–$250	$250–$350	$350–$450	over $450

*EP, BP, CP **AI, FAP, MAP
Restaurant prices are for a main course at dinner and include any taxes or service charges. Hotel prices are per night for a double room in high season, excluding taxes, service charges, and meal plans (except at all-inclusives).

GETTING THERE

Getting to Salt Cay can sometimes feel like an adventure in itself. Air Turks & Caicos sometimes cancels flights or changes flight times on a whim; in a pinch you can take a charter flight from Provo to Salt Cay on Global Air, but this is only cost-effective for groups, since you pay by the flight, not per person. There's a twice-weekly ferry from Grand Turk to Salt Cay (weather permitting). But if you are on Grand Turk and want to travel before the ferry is scheduled, ask at the dive shops to see if someone can take you over in a private boat. To get back to Grand Turk from Salt Cay, ask Debbie at Salt Cay Divers. The 30- to 40-minute boat trip typically costs $250 to $300, but the weather can sometimes put a damper on your travel plans. Once

SALT CAY BEST BETS

Beaches. Bar none, North Beach is the best on Salt Cay. Although getting to the beach is not easy, the beach itself is 3 miles of pure bliss, with bright white sand, absolutely no rocks or seaweed, glowing neon-blue water, and views of Grand Turk. It's usually deserted, and offers the island's best opportunities for off-beach snorkeling and whale-watching.

Exploring by golf cart. A rented golf cart is a fun way to get out and explore on your own. There's only one named street here, so getting around is easy—and anyone you meet can give you directions. Driving through the salt flats to North Beach is an adventure in itself, and stopping for donkeys to cross the road adds to the charm.

Clamming and pirates. Have your kids collect clams in the shallows for an experience they won't soon forget. It's fun for adults too. Candy from Pirate's Hideaway will help you search. When you're done clamming, head down Victoria Street in search of pirate graves (sometimes only marked by a pile of stones).

Hanging with the locals. Since the island has a population of 63, chances are pretty good you will meet at least a third of them during your visit. Don't be surprised if someone steps out to greet you on your explorations. Soon you'll be moving between Coral Reef Bar & Grill and Island Thyme Bistro, and you'll meet everyone there is to meet.

Doing absolutely nothing. The best days on Salt Cay are those when you do nothing at all. You can sleep in, read a book, walk around, have a lazy lunch, take a nap, snorkel a little, bird-watch, take pictures, take another nap, feed the donkeys, go beachcombing, maybe take another nap. You may be so busy doing nothing that you'll forget to check your e-mail.

you reach Salt Cay, you can rent a golf cart from Candy at Pirate's Hideaway, where you can pay by credit card.

ESSENTIALS

Air Travel **Air Turks & Caicos** (☎649/941–5481 ⊕www.airturksandcaicos.com). **Global Air** (✉Old Airport Rd., Airport,Providenciales ☎649/941–3222 ⊕www.GlobalAirways.tc).**Salt Cay Airport** (SLX ☎649/496–4999). **Salt Cay Ferry** (☎649/946–6909 ⊕www.turks andcaicoswhalewatching.com).

PLANNING YOUR TIME

Only 2½ square mi (6 square km), Salt Cay is so small that you can practically walk around it and soak up its charms in a couple of hours, but you'll have more fun if you rent a golf cart and take your time, ideally spending at least one night on the island. Start at Island Thyme Bistro, whose owner, Porter Williams, is the know-all of Salt Cay. He will provide an orientation package, information about island activities, and if you wish, a box lunch to take to the scenic coastline—where there's whale-watching in season. Try to meet Nick, Candy's brother from Pirates Hideaway; he'll show you pirate graves and the best spots to see beautiful North Beach. If you dive, make an appointment with Debbie of Salt Cay Divers to show you the wrecks. Be sure to drive past the abandoned Governor's Mansion. You'll notice that the walls around each home have embedded conch shells to keep out the donkeys and cows—you'll find yourself stopping frequently for the friendly donkeys, who rule the roads. End your night listening to Gary Stedman play at Coral Reef Bar and Grill. If it's pizza night, head back to Island Thyme Bistro; Porter makes great pizza. If Salt Cay lacks natural beauty, it definitely does not lack character (or is it that it has characters?). By the end of your stay, you will have made some lifelong friends.

WHAT TO SEE

Balfour Town. What little development there is on Salt Cay is found here. It's home to several small hotels and a few cozy stores, as well as the main dock and the Coral Reef Bar & Grill, where locals hang out with tourists to watch the sunset and drink a beer.

The grand stone **White House,** which once belonged to a wealthy salt merchant, is testimony to the heyday of Salt Cay's eponymous industry. Still privately owned by the descendants of the original family, it's sometimes opened up for tours. It's worth asking your guesthouse or hotel owner—or any local passerby—if Salt Cay islander "Uncle Lionel" is on-island, as he may give you a personal tour to see the still-intact, original furnishings, books, and medicine cabinet that date back to the early 1800s. ✉ *Victoria St., Balfour Town.*

The Versatile Islander

On an island this small almost every local must be a jack-of-all-trades. Since everything has to be imported and flown in (even the people), you will find that locals have become very resourceful. Chances are the singer in the band you are listening to during dinner was also your dive master earlier in the day. Your tour guide might be the hotel's electri-cian. The cab driver you meet on arrival at the airport might also be your boat captain on an excursion later in the day, and the check-in clerk at the airport counter might sell you the jewelry she makes at one of the little beachside shops. After a day or two, you will start recognizing people everywhere from all the different things they can do.

WHERE TO EAT

At press time, the Greenflash Café had not yet been rebuilt after destruction by Hurricane Ike; when it's back in operation it will no doubt again be an excellent place for wings and watching the sunset.

$$ ✕ Coral Reef Bar and Grill. This small restaurant sits on a beachside deck. It's colorfully painted in red, yellow, and sky-blue, and the people who hang out here are colorful, too. Have a grilled hamburger or the catch of the day, and you'll get to know the locals. The restaurant offers free Wi-Fi, so you can check your e-mail while you whale-watch and eat. On most Sundays the island turns out for rib night. In the evening you can drink beer while listening to a local dive master play guitar and sing. Then you can call it night. ✉ Victoria St., Balfour Town ☎649/241–1009 ▵Reservations essential ▭ MC, V.

$–$$ ✕ Island Thyme Bistro. Owner Porter Williams serves potent
★ alcoholic creations as well as fairly sophisticated local and international cuisine. Try steamed, freshly caught snapper in a pepper-wine sauce with peas and rice, or spicy-hot chicken curry served with tangy chutneys. Don't forget to order the "Porter" house steak (named after the owner?). You can take cooking lessons from the chef, enjoy the nightly Filipino fusion tapas during happy hour, and join the gang for Friday-night pizza. This is a great place to make friends and the best place to catch up on island gossip. The airy, trellis-covered spot overlooks the salinas. There's a small

shop with gifts and tourist information; you can also get a manicure or pedicure here. ⊠*North District* ☎*649/946–6977* ⚛*Reservations essential* ⊟*MC, V* ⊘*Closed Wed. from mid-May–June and Sept.–late Oct.*

$–$$ ✕**Pat's Place.** Island native Pat Simmons can give you a lesson in the medicinal qualities of her garden plants and periwinkle flowers as well as provide excellent native cuisine for a very reasonable price in her typical Salt Cay home. Home cooking doesn't get any closer to home than this. Try conch fritters for lunch and steamed grouper with okra rice for dinner. Be sure to call ahead, as she cooks only when there's someone to cook for. Pat now has a small grocery shop selling staples. ⊠*South District* ☎*649/946–6919* ⚛*Reservations essential* ⊟*No credit cards.*

WHERE TO STAY

$ ⌂**Genesis Beach House.** One of the newer properties on Salt Cay is in a great location near the boat dock at the end of Victoria Street, within walking distance of almost everything in and around Balfour Town. You can rent a golf cart and explore the rest of the island. The two side-by-side beach houses are close to North Beach, the island's best, and also include a private stretch of beach. Here you can enjoy rustic island life without giving up creature comforts (such as air-conditioning—though it's only in the bedrooms). **Pros:** convenient location on Victoria Street; satellite TV (though in only one of the villas); you can feed the friendly donkeys here. **Cons:** private beachfront is rocky; a/c is only in bedrooms; only one bathroom. ⊠*Victoria St., Balfour Town* ⊕*www.GenesisBeachHouse.com* ➳*2 villas, each with 2 bedrooms and 1 bath* ⚛*No a/c (some), kitchen, no TV (some), Wi-Fi, beachfront, bicycles, laundry facilities, some pets allowed, no smoking* ⊟*AE, MC, V* ☞*1-week min. EP.*

$–$$ ⌂**Pirate's Hideaway & Blackbeard's Quarters.** Owner Candy Herwin—true to her self-proclaimed pirate status—has smuggled artistic treasures across the ocean and created her own masterpieces to deck out this lair. Quirkily decorated rooms show her original style and sense of humor. The African and Crow's Nest suites have private baths; Blackbeard's Quarters is a four-bedroom house with rooms that can be rented separately but share a living room and kitchen (one room has an en suite bath; the others share a single bath). On a good day Candy will cook, but only if you entertain her and other guests—whether by reading a sonnet or singing a song. If you love eclectic and artistic surroundings and want to meet a true pirate queen, this could well be your perfect hideaway. A freshwater pool and gym have been recently added. You can rent golf carts to drive around the island in. **Pros:** artist workshops are offered during peak season. **Cons:** not directly on the beach. ✉ *Victoria St., South District* ☎ *649/946–6909* ⊕ *www. saltcay.tc* ⇨ *2 suites, 1 house* ⚷ *In-room: no a/c (some), no phone, kitchen (some). In-hotel: beachfront, water sports, bicycles* ☰ *MC, V* ⊙ *EP.*

$–$$ 🛅 **Purple Conch House.** Rustic yet charming, basic yet comfortable, this colorful and airy villa ensures a comfortable yet affordable stay (you get a significant discount with the weekly rates). One block from Victoria Street and near the beach, it's in an ideal location just across from Island Thyme Bistro and Nettie's Grocery Store, where you can pick up toiletries and the best bread on the island. The conchs embedded on the walls are painted purple, hence the name. Made for lazy days sitting on the patio watching the cows and donkeys walk by, it is a great place to de-stress. The owners don't accept credit-card payments directly, but you can use MasterCard or Visa via Paypal if you don't want to pay by check. **Pros:** central location close to everything in town; colorful and charming; across the street from Nettie's Grocery Store. **Cons:** very basic accommodations; no TV or air-conditioning; only one bathroom. ✉ *1 block from Victoria St., Balfour Town* ⊕ *www.purpleconch.com* ⇨ *2 bedrooms, 1 bath* ⚷ *No a/c, no phone, no TV, bicycles* ☰ *No credit cards* ⊙ *EP.*

$–$$ 🛅 **Tradewinds Guest Suites.** Yards away from Dean's Dock, a grove of whispering casuarina trees surrounds these five single-story, basic apartments, which offer a moderate-budget option on Salt Cay with the option of dive packages. Screened porches, hammocks overlooking the small dock, and the friendly staff are the best features. With a repair from Hurricane Ike damage, a new ceiling and new decor add to your stay. **Pros:** walking distance to diving, fishing, dining, and dancing. **Cons:** a/c is not included in basic rate; some may feel isolated with few nighttime activities and no TV. ✉ *Victoria St., Balfour Town* ☎ *649/946–6906* ⊕ *www.tradewinds.tc* ⇨ *5 apartments* ⚷ *In-room: no phone, kitchen (some), no TV. In-hotel: beachfront, water sports, bicycles* ☰ *MC, V* ⊙ *EP.*

5

$$$$ ⊞**Villas of Salt Cay.** One of the nicest and newest places to stay in Salt Cay is centrally located on Victoria Street. With its beachfront and one of the few pools on the island, the cluster of homes can comfortably sleep two to 16 people. The two-story main house, Villa Frangipani, has a TV and a colorful kitchen with a painted counter bar; ceilings are high and let the breeze come through. The separate one-bedroom cottage, Villa Olivewood, is attached by a trellis and has a separate living area and efficiency kitchen. Three attached cabanas are set up like hotel rooms, each with its own porch facing the beach and a small kitchenette. The shared private pool with its huge patio is a great gathering place after a hot day in the sun. It's an easy walk from here to listen to a band at Coral Reef Bar & Grill or to pizza night at Island Thyme. Daily maid service is included, and a cook can be brought in for an extra fee; the owner will help you with provisioning if you want to eat in. It's possible to rent the entire complex or each unit individually. **Pros:** bedrooms are set up for extra privacy; on Victoria Street within walking distance to everything; on a private stretch of beach. **Cons:** no a/c; cabanas don't have kitchens. ✉ *Victoria St., Balfour Town* ☎*649/946–6909* ⊕*www. SaltCayVilla.com* ⌕*1 2-bedroom villa, 1 1-bedroom apartment, 3 cabana suites* ♿ *no a/c, kitchen, DVD (some), Wi-Fi . In-hotel: pool, beachfront, laundry service, Wi-Fi* ▭ *MC, V* ⵏⵊ*EP.*

BEACHES

★ The north coast of Salt Cay has superb beaches, with tiny, pretty shells and weathered sea glass, but **North Beach** is the reason to visit Salt Cay; it might be the finest beach in Turks and Caicos, if not the world. Part of the beauty lies not just in the soft, powdery sand and bright blue water but in its isolation; it's very likely that you will have this lovely beach all to yourself.

Accessible by boat with the on-island tour operators, **Big Sand Cay,** 7 mi (11 km) south of Salt Cay, is tiny and totally uninhabited, but it's also known for its long, unspoiled stretches of open sand.

SPORTS & THE OUTDOORS

DIVING & SNORKELING

Scuba divers can explore the wreck of the *Endymion,* a 140-foot wooden-hull British warship that sank in 1790; you can swim through the hull and spot cannons and anchors. It's off the southern point of Salt Cay. **Salt Cay Divers** (✉ *Balfour Town* ☎ *649/946–6906* ⊕ *www.saltcaydivers.tc*) conducts daily dive trips and rents all the necessary equipment. You'll pay around $80 for a two-tank dive.

WHALE-WATCHING

During the winter months (January through April), Salt Cay is a center for whale-watching, when some 2,500 humpback whales pass close to shore. Whale-watching trips can most easily be organized through your inn or guesthouse.

SHOPPING

There was a time when the only choice for visitors was to rent a boat and head to Grand Turk for basic food supplies and sundries (or have your self-catering accommodations provide provisioning for you). Now it is easier to be self-sufficient in Salt Cay. **Nettie's Grocery Store** not only bakes fresh bread but also offers basic food supplies. **Pat's Place** now has two small shops, one with basic groceries and one with sundries. **Elouisa's** also offers some basic groceries. Ask anyone on the island where to find these small shops; the streets have no names, but it's easy to walk around the few blocks of town to find them. However, if there is anything you can't live without, the best advice is to bring it with you from home or make a grocery run in Provo and carry the food with you to Salt Cay.

For souvenirs, Salt Cay Divers has a small boutique with art prints and clothes and jewelry. The best place to buy arts and crafts is at Island Thyme Bistro; the ceiling planks are decorated with original Haitian oils that can be purchased, and Porter also sells art prints, including one of Island Thyme by famous Caribbean artist Shari Erikson. Porter also sells jewelry, T-shirts of Island Thyme, and hanging, decorative, colorful fish.

Travel Smart
Turks & Caicos

WORD OF MOUTH

"(I) noticed every day of the trip is an interesting phenomenon of the underside of the clouds appearing to be turquoise in color due to the reflection of the shallow waters of the Caicos Banks. Look for it! "

—Kristen1206

GETTING HERE & AROUND

We're proud of our Web site: Fodors.com is a great place to begin any journey. Scan Travel Wire for suggested itineraries, travel deals, restaurant and hotel openings, and other up-to-the-minute info. Check out Booking to research prices and book plane tickets, hotel rooms, rental cars, and vacation packages. Head to Talk for on-the-ground pointers from travelers who frequent our message boards. You can also link to loads of other travel-related resources.

You'll arrive on Provo by air, and then you'll need to rent or take taxis to get around. The island is flat and has no traffic lights; most places are no farther than 20 minutes away. On Grand Turk it's fun to get around by bicycle or scooter; the island is small and the roads are in good condition. On tiny Salt Cay, Parrot Cay, and Pine Cay, the preferred mode of transportation is a golf cart. There is a ferry to North Caicos; the rest of the islands require a boat or plane to reach them, though you can now drive from North Caicos to Middle Caicos.

■TIP→ Ask the local tourist board about hotel packages during the Summer Music Festival, the Fall Film Festival, and the November Conch Festival.

■ BY AIR

The main gateways into the Turks and Caicos Islands are Providenciales International Airport and Grand Turk International Airport. For private planes, Provo Air Center is a full-service FBO (Fixed Base Operator) offering refueling, maintenance, and short-term storage, as well as on-site customs and immigration clearance, a lounge, and concierge services. Even if you are going on to other islands in the chain, you will probably stop in Provo first for customs, then take a domestic flight onward.

Airlines & Airports Airline and Airport Links.com (⊕ *www. airlineandairportlinks.com*) has links to many of the world's airlines and airports.

Airline-Security Issues Transportation Security Administration (⊕ *www.tsa.gov*) has answers for almost every question that might come up.

AIRPORTS
Almost all the flights to Turks and Caicos Islands arrive in Providenciales, where all scheduled international flights land at this writing and where you will go through immigration and customs. Make sure you have all of your paperwork completely filled out, as immigration lines can be slow; in fact, you may wait 30 to 40 minutes from the time you disembark to the time you pass through customs. If you are on a private or chartered plane, you

can also go through immigration and customs at Ambergris Cay or Grand Turk. Airlines will tell you to arrive at the airport three hours before your return flight; this is a good advice in most cases, because security will inspect all your luggage by hand before allowing you to check in. During the week, two hours is probably enough time, but on Saturday or Sunday, especially during peak season, three hours is more appropriate.

Airport Information **Ambergris Cay Airport** (☎649/941–9000) **Grand Turk International Airport** (*GDT* ☎649/946–2233). **Middle Caicos Airport** (*MDS* ☎649/946–6141)**North Caicos Airport** (*NCA* 649/231–3986)**Pine Cay Airport** (*PIC*☎no phone) **Providenciales International Airport** (*PLS* ☎649/941–5670).**Salt Cay Airport** (*SLX* ☎649/496–4999)**South Caicos Airport** (*XSC* ☎649/946–4999)

GROUND TRANSPORTATION

In most cases, if you are staying at a hotel or resort there will be a representative holding a sign to greet you when you arrive in Provo; you will then be put into a regular taxi to the resort. (Only a few hotels are allowed to offer real shuttle service; most are required by law to use regular taxis.) Because Amanyara, Parrot Cay, and Nikki Beach are away from the main hub, they are allowed to transport you directly. Even if you have not made prior arrangements, there will be plenty of taxis meeting each flight. To the main area of Grace Bay Road, expect to pay around $25 per couple one-way. You can also have a car rental waiting at the airport;

all the rental car companies offer this service. If someone is picking you up, they may wait for you in the nearby small parking lot that charges $1 an hour.

On other islands there will also be taxis waiting for flights. On Pine Cay someone will pick you up in a golf cart. On Salt Cay you could walk if need be.

FLIGHTS

Although carriers and schedules can vary seasonally, there are many nonstop and connecting flights to Providenciales from several U.S. cities on American, Delta, and USAirways. There are also flights from other parts of the Caribbean on Air Turks & Caicos; this airline also flies to some of the smaller islands in the chain from Provo. There are also flights from Nassau on Bahamas Air.

Airline Contacts **Air Turks & Caicos** (☎649/941–5481 ⊕www. airturksandcaicos.com). **American Airlines** (☎649/946–4948 or 800/433–7300 ⊕www.aa.com). **Bahamas Air** (☎242/377–5505 in Nassau or 800/222–4262 ⊕ up.bahamasair.com).**Delta** (☎800/241–4141 ⊕www.delta. com). **USAirways** (☎800/622–1015 ⊕www.usairways.com).

CHARTER FLIGHTS

One charter company can fly you from Provo to anywhere that you need to go in the Turks and Caicos (or the Caribbean for that matter). Sometimes a charter may be the only practical way to get to Salt Cay, since Air Turks and Caicos is not very reliable. Global Air can be expensive since you pay per flight, not by the passenger. However, if a group of you are going to a smaller island, it is the best way to go.

Contacts Global Air (✉ *Old Airport Rd., Airport* ☎ *649/941–3222* ⊕ *www.GlobalAirways.tc*).

▌ BY BOAT & FERRY

Daily scheduled ferry service from Caribbean Cruisin' began in 2007 between Provo and North Caicos, with several departures from Walkin Marina in Leeward.

There's a twice-weekly ferry from Salt Cay to Grand Turk (weather permitting).

Contacts Caribbean Cruisin' (✉ *Walkin Marina, Leeward, Providenciales* ☎ *649/946–5406* or *649/231–4191* ⊕ *tcimall.tc/northcaicos/images/ferryservice.pdf caribbeancruisin@gmail.com*). **Salt Cay Ferry** (☎ *649/946–6909* ⊕ *www.turksandcaicoswhalewatching.com*).

▌ BY CAR

You may or may not be able to get by without a rental car in Provo, depending on where you're staying. It's wise to plan on renting a car for at least a couple of days for exploring, then deciding whether you need it the rest of the week. Taxis can be expensive, with each ride equaling the cost of a daily rental, but if you feel uncomfortable driving on the left or if you want to go out and not worry about having too much to drink, then a taxi can be a good option. A car is the way to go if you want to do much exploring, since taxis will not wait for you in isolated areas.

You will also need a car if you plan to snorkel at Smith's Reef, where you won't be able to call a taxi.

If you travel to North Caicos or Middle Caicos, you almost have to rent a car, because everything is so spread out. On the other islands, you can get by just walking or taking an occasional taxi.

To rent, you do need to have a valid U.S. license to drive, and you need to be 25 or older; no international or local license is required.

GASOLINE

Gasoline is expensive, much more so than in the United States. Expect to pay about $2 to $3 more a gallon than you would at home. The good news? Each island is small enough that you probably won't use a full tank, even if you keep your rental car for a full week. There are numerous gas stations around Provo, but most accept only cash. The Texaco on Leeward Highway at the roundabout to Seven Stars is the only one that takes credit cards.

PARKING

Parking in the Turks and Caicos is easy. There are paved public accesses to all the beaches on Provo. Grace Bay has numerous public parking lots up and down its 12 miles. You will find even the secluded beaches have areas to leave your car. All the resorts and restaurants offer free parking; even the resorts that are gated have general public areas to park.

North and Middle Caicos also have parking areas at all the restaurants and places to stay. You probably won't have a car on any of the other islands, but all the hotels have some free parking spots.

RENTAL CARS

Avis and Budget have offices on the islands. You might also try local agencies such as Grace Bay Car Rentals, Rent a Buggy, and Tropical Auto Rentals in Provo.

Pelican Car Rentals is on North Caicos.

Small cars start at around $39 per day, and a small high-clearance vehicle averages about $69 a day. All rental agencies in the Turks and Caicos will drop off a car for you at either the airport or your hotel. Upon return, you can always leave it at the airport. All the companies are fairly competitive and offer similar rates. All the companies offer cars with the steering wheel on the left (as in the U.S.) except for Grace Bay Car Rentals, which carries right-drive cars (as in the UK).

Contacts Avis (⊠ *Providenciales* ☎ 649/946–4705 ⊕ *www.avis. tc*). **Budget** (⊠ *Providenciales* ☎ 649/946–4079 ⊕ *www.provo.net/ budget*). **Grace Bay Car Rentals** (⊠ *Providenciales* ☎ 649/941–8500 ⊕ *www.gracebaycarrentals.com*). **Pelican Car Rentals** (⊠ *North Caicos* ☎ 649/241–8275). **Rent a Buggy** (⊠ *Providenciales* ☎ 649/946–4158 ⊕ *www.rent-abuggy.tc*). **Scooter Bob's** (⊠ *Turtle Cove, Providenciales* ☎ 649/946–4684 ⊕ *www.Provo.net/Scooter*). **Tony's Car Rental** (⊠ *Grand Turk* ☎ 649/946–1879 ⊕ *www.Tonys CarRental.com*). **Tropical Auto Rentals** (⊠ *Providenciales* ☎ 649/946–5300 ⊕ *www.provo.net/tropicalauto*).

RENTAL CAR INSURANCE

Everyone who rents a car wonders whether the insurance that the rental companies offer is worth the expense. No one—including us—has a simple answer. If you own a car, your personal auto insurance may cover a rental to some degree, though not all policies protect you abroad; always read your policy's fine print. If you don't have auto insurance, then seriously consider buying the collision- or loss-damage waiver (CDW or LDW) from the car-rental company, which eliminates your liability for damage to the car. Some credit cards offer CDW coverage, but it's usually supplemental to your own insurance and rarely covers SUVs, minivans, luxury models, and the like. If your coverage is secondary, you may still be liable for loss-of-use costs from the car-rental company. But no credit-card insurance is valid unless you use that card for *all* transactions, from reserving to paying the final bill. All companies exclude car rental in some countries, so be sure to find out about the destination to which you are traveling. It's sometimes cheaper to buy insurance as part of your general travel insurance policy.

ROADSIDE EMERGENCIES

Discuss with the rental-car agency what to do in the case of an emergency, as this sometimes differs between companies. Make sure you understand what your insurance covers and what it doesn't, and what the car company's policies are. If you find yourself stranded, chances are you'll be close to somewhere where you can ask for help, or someone sooner or later will go by that has a cell phone. Most rental companies have after-hours cell phones, and will either show up to help or bring you a new car. Keep emergency numbers (car-rental agency and your accommodation) with you, just in case. Picking up hitchhikers is not recommended.

ROAD CONDITIONS

Major reconstruction of Leeward Highway on Providenciales has been completed, and most of the road is now a four-lane divided highway complete with round-abouts. However, the paved two-lane roads through the settlements on Providenciales can be quite rough, although signage is improving. A high-clearance vehicle is recommended if you want to head to Malcolm's Beach or if you are staying in the Turtle Tail area, those two areas have roads of rolled pack sand and have been known to have many potholes. The roads on the entire chain of islands have recently been paved; some even have curbing to avoid potholes. The less-traveled roads in Grand Turk and the family islands are, in general, smooth and paved.

RULES OF THE ROAD

Driving here is on the left side of the road, British style; when pulling out into traffic; remember to look to your right. Give way to anyone entering a roundabout, as round-abouts are still a relatively new concept in the Turks & Caicos; stop even if you are on what appears to be the primary road. And take them slowly; locals are quite used to seeing tourists and

will keep their distance if they see you are struggling. The maximum speed is 40 mph (64 kph), 20 mph (30 kph) through settlements, and limits, as well as the use of seat belts, are enforced. Use extra caution at night, especially if you've had some drinks and don't remember to drive on the left. While the police might not necessarily stop you, if you wreck you may have to be flown (expensively) to Miami. You will also be responsible for a new car. Don't be surprised if the car in front of you all of the sudden stops to say hello to someone, so always be on guard.

▌ BY TAXI

Taxis (actually large vans) on Providenciales are metered, and rates are regulated by the government at $2 per person per mile traveled. In Provo call the Provo Taxi & Bus Group for more information. On the family islands (i.e., the smaller, outlying islands other than Provo), taxis may not be metered, so it's usually best to try to negotiate a cost for your trip in advance

On Provo, expect to pay around $25 per couple one way from the airport to most resorts; children often only pay half price—but always ask first, some charge half, some full price. You may also be charge extra for baggage, so always ask. Unless you have a rental car waiting for you at the airport, you will be taken to your resort by taxi (no Grace Bay resorts are allowed to offer airport shuttles), even if you are greeted by a hotel representative. If you are using a taxi as your primary mode of transportation, get your driver's direct cell number. You will have to call for service, as they don't usually hang out anywhere except the airport. Taxi drivers are a great source of information about the islands, especially any political gossip, so if you find a good driver it's advisable to keep calling him directly. It's customary to tip about 10% per ride.

Contact Provo Taxi & Bus Group (☎649/946–5481).

ESSENTIALS

■ ACCOMMODATIONS

Accommodation options in the Turks & Caicos are seemingly endless, and though there's a wide range of price options, your accommodations will likely be your greatest expense. However, if you're prepared for this, you can find some unusual and memorable lodging experiences. There are many gorgeous villas in every size to choose from. Most of the resorts are made up of individually owned condos (not time-shares, but rather fully owned condominium units) placed in the hotel's rental pool when the owners are not in residence. Providenciales has two all-inclusive resorts: the family-oriented Beaches, and the adults-only Club Med. There is only one time-share on the island, and it has a three-year waiting list for trade-ins. The outer islands have more basic and rustic accommodations.

■TIP→ Assume that hotels operate on the European Plan (**EP**, no meals) unless you specify that they use the Breakfast Plan (**BP**, with full breakfast), Continental Plan (**CP**, continental breakfast), Full American Plan (**FAP**, all meals), or Modified American Plan (**MAP**, breakfast and dinner), or are all-inclusive (**AI**, all meals and most activities).

For lodging price categories, consult the price charts found near the beginning of each chapter.

T&C LODGING TIPS

Budget for the add-ons. You must pay 10% V.A.T., plus an additional 10% service charge.

Avoid peak season. Rates are about 35% higher from mid-December through mid-April.

Book in advance. Especially during peak season some resorts fill up quickly with repeat visitors.

Reservations required. You cannot enter the Turks & Caicos unless you have reserved a place to stay.

Construction warning. If you're looking for some peace and quiet, ask if there is any construction next to the resort.

Book direct. You can sometimes get rates that are just as good (if not better) by booking directly through the resort.

Know the terminology. An "ocean view" may require you to stand on your tippy toes at the right angle. Some "garden view" rooms are just as nice for a better price.

Consider your options. Pampering is expensive; if you're low-maintenance, consider a self-catering apartment that will save you money on both food and resort services.

Not sure where to stay? Subscribe to *Where When How?* magazine before you go.

APARTMENT & HOUSE RENTALS

Villa and condo rentals are quite common in the Turks & Caicos; in fact, they make up the majority of accommodations. On Provo most villas are ultra luxurious getaways, and have the prices to match. On the smaller islands, villas are basic and comfortable and tend to be more economical alternatives. Private apartment rentals can save you money but tend to be more residential, with fewer services. On any of the islands they are easy to book, and management companies will send a representative to meet you at the airport and lead the way.

Contacts Forgetaway (⊕ www.forgetaway.weather.com). **Home Away** (☎ 512/493—0382 in U.S. ⊕ www.homeaway.com). **Vacation Rentals by Owner** (VRBO ⊕ www.VRBO.com). **Villas International** (☎ 415/499—9490 or 800/221—2260 in U.S. ⊕ www.villasintl.com).

HOTELS

Hotels and resorts in Turks and Caicos run the gamut from small inns with basic accommodations to full-service, private-island resorts. There are a few classy boutique hotels on Provo, but only three chain hotels. Parrot Cay and the Meridian Club on Pine Cay are private-island resorts with all the pampering and privileges you'd expect for the high prices.

▌ COMMUNICATIONS

INTERNET

The majority of resorts throughout the Turks & Caicos offer Wi-Fi service in their public areas, if not in the rooms, so you can keep up with

---

FODORS.COM CONNECTION

Before your trip, be sure to check-out what other travelers are saying in Talk on www.fodors.com.

---

e-mail and the Internet. There are also several Internet cafés, including TCI Online Internet Cafe in the Ports of Call shopping center on Provo; the center offers an all-day plan and also rents cell phones.

Contacts TCI Online Internet Cafe (⊠ Ports of Call, Grace Bay Rd, Grace Bay ☎ 649/941—4711).

PHONES

The country code for the Turks & Caicos is 649. To call the Turks & Caicos from the U.S., dial 1 plus the 10-digit number, which includes 649. Be aware that this is an international call. Calls from the islands are expensive, and many hotels add steep surcharges for long distance. Talk fast.

CALLING WITHIN THE DESTINATION

To make local calls, just dial the seven-digit number. Most hotels and resorts charge for local calls, usually 50¢ a minute. Ask at the front desk if you need to dial "9" to get a dial tone; some require this for a line, other places you just dial directly.

CALLING OUTSIDE THE DESTINATION

To call the U.S., dial 1, then the area code, and the seven-number. Remember that this is still an international call and will be charged accordingly.

CALLING CARDS

Calling cards are not recommended in Turks and Caicos, not even for international calls. They are hard to use, and you are charged even for toll-free connection numbers. It's actually cheaper to buy a simple "pay as you go" cell phone or a SIM card for your own unlocked mobile phone when you arrive.

MOBILE PHONES

If you have a multiband phone (some countries use frequencies different from those used in the United States) and your service provider uses the world-standard GSM network (as do T-Mobile, Cingular, and Verizon), you can probably use your phone abroad. Roaming fees can be steep, however: 99¢ a minute is considered reasonable. And overseas you normally pay the toll charges for incoming calls. It's almost always cheaper to send a text message than to make a call, since text messages have a very low set fee (often less than 5¢).

Many U.S.–based cell phones work in the Turks & Caicos; use your own or rent one from Lime. AT&T works well on Provo, but Verizon does not have consistently good coverage. All telephone service—both traditional and mobile—is provided by Lime and Digicel. Local cell-phone coverage is very good; you'll even get reception on the uninhabited cays. (Be aware, however, that Lime charges you for an international call when you dial a U.S. toll-free number from the Turks and Caicos.)

If you just want to make local calls, consider buying a new SIM

card (note that your provider may have to unlock your phone for you to use a different SIM card) and a prepaid service plan in the destination. You'll then have a local number and can make local calls at local rates. If your trip is extensive, you could also simply buy a new cell phone in your destination, as the initial cost will be offset over time.

■TIP→**If you travel internationally frequently, save one of your old mobile phones or buy a cheap one on the Internet; ask your cell phone company to unlock it for you, and take it with you as a travel phone, buying a new SIM card with pay-as-you-go service in each destination.**

Contacts **Digicel TCI** (⊕*www. digiceltci.com*). **Lime** (☎*649/946– 2200, 800/744–7777 for long distance, 649/266–6328 for Internet access, 811 for mobile service* ⊕*www.time4lime.com*). **Mobal** (☎*888/888–9162* ⊕*www.mobalrental.com*). **Planet Fone** (☎*888/988– 4777* ⊕*www.planetfone.com*).

▌ CUSTOMS & DUTIES

Customs in the Turks and Caicos is very straightforward and simple. On the flight you will receive two forms. The first is your customs declaration, and you should fill out one per family. The second form is a Turks & Caicos Embarkation and Disembarkation Form, which each person must fill out. Both forms must be filled out completely before you can get in the customs line. Make sure to keep the stub from the Disembarkation

Form; you'll need to show it to leave the island. If you are 17 years old or older, you are allowed to bring in free of import duty 1 liter spirits or 2 liters wine; Either 200 cigarettes *or* 100 cigarillos OR 50 cigars OR 250 grams of smoking tobacco, and 50 grams of perfume *or* 0.25 liters of eau de toilette. If you have $10,000 or more in cash you must declare it.

The immigration entrance lines can be long, especially when several planes arrive in quick succession. Make sure you have filled the forms completely before you get off the plane.

Turks and Caicos Islands Information TCI Tourism (⊕ *www.Turks andCaicosTourism.com*).

U.S. Information U.S. Customs and Border Protection (⊕ *www. cbp.gov*).

▌EATING OUT

The Turks and Caicos has almost any kind of restaurant you want, especially Provo. From small beach shacks to gorgeous upscale dining rooms and everything in between, this destination is a gastronomical delight. There are cafés and delis, international restaurants, and some of the best chefs in the Caribbean; what you won't find is fast food or restaurant chains. Typically, the restaurants offer very wide choices, so even vegetarians and picky eaters will find something appealing on most menus. If a restaurant does not have a children's menu, the chef will usually be willing to make something to suit your kids, so don't be afraid to ask. Restau-

WORD OF MOUTH

Was the service stellar or not up to snuff? Did the food give you shivers of delight or leave you cold? Did the prices and portions make you happy or sad? Rate restaurants and write your own reviews in Travel Ratings or start a discussion about your favorite places in Travel Talk on www. fodors.com. Your comments might even appear in our books. Yes, you, too, can be a correspondent!

rants cater primarily to American tastes. Dinner usually starts a little later than Americans are used to; most restaurants are full by 8, and after dinner they are also the nightlife venues in this sleepy destination. Just bring a full wallet; most restaurants are upscale and expensive, though you will also find a few slightly less expensive, more casual options. A typical meal averages $80 to $120 per couple without a bottle of wine, even more if you add that in.

Unless otherwise noted, restaurants listed in this guide are open daily for lunch and dinner.

TURKS & CAICOS CUISINE

The most typical foods on these islands come from the sea. Grouper and snapper are usually the catch of the day, often grilled with jerk spices and sauces. Grouper is used in fish tacos at Hemingway's, giving a Caribbean twist to Mexican food. In season, spiny lobster is grabbed fresh from the ocean (the lobster Thermidor at Coyaba is insanely delicious). One favorite food in the Turks and Caicos is conch; so loved is this white meat from the sea that it even has its own festival in November, with recipe and tasting competitions. Conch is made every way imaginable, including in sushi. Macaroni and cheese or peas with rice are common side dishes, especially in spots that serve more local food. Coleslaw here even has a Caribbean twist, often including pineapple or mango. For a typical island breakfast, order broiled fish with baked beans and grits.

PAYING

Most major credit cards (Visa, American Express, Discover, and MasterCard—Diner's Club less so) are accepted in restaurants. If a place takes cash only, it's noted on the review.

For dining price categories, consult the price charts found near the beginning of each chapter. For guidelines on tipping see Tipping, below.

RESERVATIONS & DRESS

We only mention reservations when they are essential (there's no other way you'll ever get a table) or when they are not accepted. We mention dress only when men are required to wear a jacket or a jacket and tie. While you don't need fancy dresses or even long pants at most places, you will look out of place in T-shirts, jeans, and tennis shoes.

WINES, BEER & SPIRITS

Major brands of liquor are widely available in the Turks and Caicos, but you may want to bring a bottle of your favorite with you, as there are no real duty-free bargains to be had. Imported U.S.

beer is particularly expensive; a case of Bud Light or Miller Light can run around $40. For beer lovers, it's always fun to try something new: the brewery for Turks Head, which is a heavier-tasting beer than its American counterparts, offers tours. Caicos rum is also made in the Turks and Caicos. A new Turks and Caicos Rum, called Bamberra Rum has just been launched; it's a smooth blend of the best rums in the Caribbean, and a bargain compared to other rums. Some Caribbean brands are available in local stores, including Kalik and Red Stripe. Remember that while you can always buy alcohol at a bar, it is against the law to purchase it from a store on a Sunday.

▮ ELECTRICITY

Electricity is fairly stable throughout the islands, and the current is suitable for all U.S. appliances (120/240 volts, 60 Hz).

▮ EMERGENCIES

The emergency numbers in the Turks & Caicos are 999 or 911.

▮ HEALTH

Turks and Caicos is a very safe and healthy destination. The tap water may not be the best tasting, but it is safe to drink. Food-safety standards are high, and you rarely hear of upset stomachs or outbreaks of food poisoning. At this writing the Turks and Caicos do not have any major mosquito-born illnesses like dengue fever, which has been a problem on many Caribbean islands, but there are no-see-ums at dusk, and they really like to bite your ankles. Grace Bay Beach is usually clean and clear of any pests. Occasionally you'll run across a stray stingray; make sure not to step on its tail and you'll be fine. There are no poisonous snakes in the Turks and Caicos.

OVER-THE-COUNTER REMEDIES

Most of the supplies are similar to those in the U.K., U. S., and Canada. You will find all the major brands that you are used too readily available around Provo, though you will find that prices are higher than at home. Over-the-counter drugs can be found at pharmacies and supermarkets, and even at small convenience stores. If you plan to travel beyond Provo, however, you may wish to stock up on necessities. Supplies may be slimmer in the less-developed islands. Sunscreen is especially expensive in the Grace Bay area; it's much more reasonably priced at the IGA supermarket. If you need bug spray, get something with at least 25% DEET; Off-brand spray is readily available. If you forget to buy it and find yourself at dusk with no-see-ums biting, ask your servers at the restaurant; there's a good chance they'll have a bottle on hand.

Health Warnings National Centers for Disease Control & Prevention (*CDC* ☎ *877/394–8747 international travelers' health line* ⊕ *www.cdc.gov/travel*). **World Health Organization** (*WHO* ⊕ *www.who.int*).

▌ HOURS OF OPERATION

Banks are typically open Monday through Friday from 9 to 4. Post offices are open weekdays from 10 to 4. Shops are generally open weekdays from 10 to 5 or 6; most shops are closed on Sundays. You cannot buy alcohol anywhere in the islands on Sunday except at a bar or restaurant.

HOLIDAYS

Public holidays are New Year's Day, Commonwealth Day (second Monday in March), Good Friday, Easter Monday, National Heroes Day (last Monday in May), Queen's Birthday (third Monday in June), Emancipation Day (first Monday in August), National Youth Day (last Monday in September), Columbus Day (second Monday in October), International Human Rights Day (last Monday in October), Christmas Day, and Boxing Day (December 26).

▌ MAIL

The post office is in downtown Provo at the corner of Airport Road (stamp collectors will be interested in the wide selection of stamps sold by the Philatelic Bureau). You'll pay 50¢ to send a postcard to the U.S., 60¢ to Canada and the UK; letters, per ½ ounce, cost 60¢ to the United States, 80¢ to Canada and the UK. When writing to the Turks & Caicos Islands; be sure to include the specific island and "Turks & Caicos Islands, BWI" (British West Indies). In general, the post office is not very reliable, and packages take an especially long time to arrive. There is no home delivery of mail;

everyone has a PO Box. Expect post cards to take a month to get to your friends and neighbors—if they get them at all.

SHIPPING PACKAGES

FedEx has offices on Provo and Grand Turk. Though expensive, FedEx should be the only way to send something to the islands. Keep in mind that buildings aren't numbered, though everyone on the island knows where each place is. Villas have names and not numbers, and there is no home delivery on any of the islands (even by FedEx); people must pick up packages at the FedEx office.

Contacts **FedEx** (☎649/946–4682 on Provo). **Philatelic Bureau** (☎649/946–1534).

▌ MONEY

Prices quoted in this chapter are in U.S. dollars, which is the official currency in the islands.

Major credit cards and traveler's checks are accepted at many establishments. Bring small-denomination bills to the less populated islands—but bring enough cash to hold you over; many of the smaller islands deal in cash only and have no ATMs. Some islands don't even have banks, so get some cash while on Provo if heading elsewhere.

Prices throughout this guide are given for adults. Substantially reduced fees are almost always available for children, students, and senior citizens.

ATMS & BANKS

On Provo, there are ATMs at all bank branches (Scotiabank and First Caribbean), at the Graceway IGA Supermarket, at Ports of Call shopping center, and at Ocean Club Plaza. There are also Scotiabank and First Caribbean branches on Grand Turk.

CREDIT CARDS

Throughout this guide, the following abbreviations are used: **AE,** American Express; **D,** Discover; **DC,** Diners Club; **MC,** MasterCard; and **V,** Visa.

It's a good idea to inform your credit-card company before you travel, especially if you're going abroad and don't travel internationally very often. Otherwise, the credit-card company might put a hold on your card owing to unusual activity—not a good thing halfway through your trip. Record all your credit-card numbers—as well as the phone numbers to call if your cards are lost or stolen—in a safe place, so you're prepared should something go wrong. All the major credit card companies have general numbers you can call (collect if you're abroad) if your card is lost, but you're better off calling the number of your issuing bank, since MasterCard and Visa usually just transfer you to your bank; your bank's number is usually printed on your card.

If you plan to use your credit card for cash advances, you'll need to apply for a PIN at least two weeks before your trip. Although it's usually cheaper (and safer) to use a credit card abroad for large purchases (so you can cancel payments or be reimbursed if there's a problem), note that some credit-card companies *and* the banks that issue them add substantial percentages to all foreign transactions, whether they're in a foreign currency or not. Check on these fees before leaving home, so there won't be any surprises when you get the bill.

In the shops, some require a $25 minimum to charge. A few shops may pass along their 3% to 5% surcharge if you pay by credit card; the clerk will tell you before you pay.

Reporting Lost Cards **American Express** (☎800/528–4800 in U.S., 336/393–1111 collect from abroad ⊕www.americanexpress.com). **MasterCard** (☎800/627–8372 in U.S., 636/722–7111 collect from abroad ⊕www.mastercard.com). **Visa** (☎800/847–2911 in U.S., 410/581–9994 collect from abroad ⊕www.visa.com).

▌ PACKING

Most accommodations in Provo have washers and dryers in the units, so pack light. You can wash your clothes conveniently at your whim and dry swimsuits before repacking. If your resort doesn't offer laundry facilities or a laundry service, you'll find a dry cleaner next to Beaches and a laundromat on Leeward Highway. Do not forget sunglasses; the sun is strong, and it's expensive to buy a new pair here. If you travel with a carry-on, airlines only allow 3-ounce bottles of liquids; don't worry, it's not too expensive to buy sunscreen at the Graceway IGA supermar-

ket. There's really not a huge bug problem in the Turks & Caicos, but sometimes after rain or at dusk you might get a bite or two, so either buy or bring some Off.

For women, sundresses are fine for the nicest restaurant, and for men tropical-print shirts will do nicely. Almost all the resorts and villas have hairdryers and give you shampoo, conditioner, and a small box of laundry detergent. "Bring half the clothes and twice the money"— words to live by.

▌ PASSPORTS & VISAS

U.S. citizens must have a valid passport to travel by air to the Turks & Caicos. Everyone must have an ongoing or return ticket and a confirmed hotel reservation. Make sure to keep the embarkation stub that you filled out when you landed, you'll need it when you leave.

▌ RESTROOMS

There are public restrooms and a playground in between Wymara and Aquamarine Beach Houses, for those times when you haven't realized how far you've walked.

▌ SAFETY

Although crime is not a major concern in the Turks & Caicos Islands, petty theft does occur here, and you're advised to leave your valuables in your hotel safe-deposit box and lock doors in cars and rooms when unattended. Small petty thefts have been known to happen, especially near construction sites (which are common, especially on Provo). Do all of the things your parents taught you: don't walk in dark areas, especially the beach at night; don't leave valuables in a car unattended; if you wouldn't do it at home, don't do it here.

■TIP→ Distribute your cash, credit cards, IDs, and other valuables between a deep front pocket, an inside jacket or vest pocket, and a hidden money pouch. Don't reach for the money pouch once you're in public.

Contact **Transportation Security Administration** (*TSA*; ⊕ *www.tsa.gov*).

General Information & Warnings **Australian Department of Foreign Affairs & Trade** (⊕ *www.smartraveller.gov.au*). **Consular Affairs Bureau of Canada** (⊕ *www.voyage.gc.ca*). **U.K. Foreign & Commonwealth Office** (⊕ *www.fco.gov.uk/travel*). **U.S. Department of State** (⊕ *www.travel.state.gov*).

▌ TAXES

The departure tax is $35 and is usually included in the cost of your airline ticket. If not, it's payable only in cash or traveler's check. Restaurants and hotels add a 10% government tax. Hotels also typically add 10% to 15% for service.

▌ TIME

The Turks and Caicos are in the Eastern Time Zone, the same as New York City and Atlanta. Unlike most Caribbean destinations, the Turks and Caicos do follow Daylight Savings Time when the U.S. does—except, oddly, at Club Med, which does not change its clocks, making them an hour earlier than

those on the rest of the island during months when Daylight Savings Time is in effect.

Time Zones **Timeanddate.com** (⊕ *www.timeanddate.com/worldclock*).

▌ TIPPING

In restaurants, check your bill to see if a 10% service charge has been added; if yes, then supplement it by 5%, or even more if service was outstanding. If no service charge has been added, then tip as you would at home, about 15%. Taxi drivers also expect a tip, about 10% of your fare.

▌ TOURS

Whether you travel by taxi, boat, or plane, you should try to venture beyond your resort's grounds and beach. The natural environment is one of the main attractions of the Turks & Caicos, yet few people explore beyond the natural wonder of the beach.

TOUR OPERATORS
Big Blue Unlimited has taken eco-touring to a whole new level with educational ecotours, including three-hour kayak trips and more-land-based guided journeys around the family islands. Their "Coastal Ecology and Wildlife" tour is a kayak adventure through red mangroves to bird habitats, rock iguana hideaways, and natural fish nurseries. The "North Caicos Mountain Bike Eco Tour" gets you on a bike to explore the island, the plantation ruins, the inland lakes, and a flamingo pond with a stop-off at Susan Butterfield's home for lunch.

Package costs range from $85 to $225 per person.

Nell's Taxi offers taxi tours of Provo, priced between $25 and $30 for the first hour and $25 for each additional hour.

Special day excursions are available from local airline Air Turks & Caicos. Trips include whale-watching in Salt Cay and trips to Middle Caicos or North Caicos that include, in addition to the flight, a map, water, lunch voucher, and a mountain bike to explore for the day. Trips start from $99, which includes round-trip air. Day-trips to Grand Turk are available with Air Turks & Caicos; for around $179, you get a round-trip flight to the capital island, a short tour, admission to the Turks & Caicos National Museum, lunch, and time to explore on your own.

Contacts Air Turks & Caicos (☎649/946–5481 or 649/946–4181 ⊕www.airturksandcaicos.com). **Big Blue Unlimited** (✉Leeward Marina, Leeward, Providenciales ☎649/946–5034 ⊕www.bigblue.tc). **Nell's Taxi** (☎649/231–0051).

▌ TRIP INSURANCE

Comprehensive travel policies typically cover trip-cancellation and interruption, letting you cancel or cut your trip short because of a personal emergency, illness, or, in some cases, acts of terrorism in your destination. Such policies also cover evacuation and medical care. Some also cover you for trip delays because of bad weather or mechanical problems as well as for lost or delayed baggage. Another

type of coverage to look for is financial default—that is, when your trip is disrupted because a tour operator, airline, or cruise line goes out of business. Generally you must buy this when you book your trip or shortly thereafter, and it's only available to you if your operator isn't on a list of excluded companies.

At the very least, consider buying medical-only coverage. Neither Medicare nor some private insurers cover medical expenses anywhere outside of the United States (including time aboard a cruise ship, even if it leaves from a U.S. port). Medical-only policies typically reimburse you for medical care (excluding that related to pre-existing conditions) and hospitalization abroad, and provide for evacuation. You still have to pay the bills and await reimbursement from the insurer, though.

Another option is to sign up with a medical-evacuation assistance company. A membership in one of these companies gets you doctor referrals, emergency evacuation or repatriation, 24-hour hotlines for medical consultation, and other assistance. International SOS Assistance Emergency and AirMed International provide evacuation services and medical referrals. MedjetAssist offers medical evacuation.

Expect comprehensive travel insurance policies to cost about 4% to 7% or 8% of the total price of your trip (it's more like 8%–12% if you're over age 70). A medical-only policy may or may not be cheaper than a comprehensive policy. Always read the fine print of your policy to make sure that you are covered for the risks that are of most concern to you. Compare several policies to make sure you're getting the best price and range of coverage available.

■TIP→ OK. You know you can save a bundle on trips to warm-weather destinations by traveling during hurricane season. But there's also a chance that a severe storm will disrupt your plans. The solution? Look for hotels and resorts that offer storm/hurricane guarantees. Although they rarely allow refunds, most guarantees do let you rebook later if a storm strikes.

Insurance Comparison Sites
Insure My Trip.com (☎800/487–4722 ⊕www.insuremytrip.com). **Square Mouth.com** (☎800/240–0369 or 727/490–5803 ⊕www. squaremouth.com).

Medical Assistance Companies
AirMed International Medical Group (⊕www.airmed.com) **International SOS** (⊕www.international sos.com). **MedjetAssist** (⊕www. medjetassist.com).

Medical-Only Insurers **International Medical Group** (☎800/628–4664 ⊕www.im-global.com). **Wallach & Company** (☎800/237–6615 or 540/687–3166 ⊕www.wallach.com).

Comprehensive Travel Insurers
Access America (☎866/729–6021 ⊕www.accessamerica.com). **AIG Travel Guard** (☎800/826–4919 ⊕www.travelguard.com). **CSA Travel Protection** (☎800/873–9855 ⊕www.csatravelprotection.com).

HTH Worldwide (☎610/254–8700 ⊕www.hthworldwide.com). **Travelex Insurance** (☎888/228–9792 ⊕www.travelex-insurance.com). **Travel Insured International** (☎800/243–3174 ⊕www.travel insured.com).

❚ VISITOR INFORMATION

The tourist offices on Grand Turk and Providenciales are open daily from 9 to 5.

Before You Leave **Turks & Caicos Islands Tourist Board** (☎954/568–6588 in Ft. Lauderdale or 800/241–0824 ⊕www.turksandcaicostourism. com).

In Turks & Caicos Islands **Turks & Caicos Islands Tourist Board** (✉Front St., Cockburn Town, Grand Turk ☎649/946–2321 ✉Stubbs Diamond Plaza, The Bight, Providenciales ☎649/946–4970 ⊕www. turksandcaicostourism.com).

ONLINE TRAVEL TOOLS

To make the most of your vacation, check out the Web site for *Where-WhenHow* magazine, which has links to everything in the Turks and Caicos and a separate Web site for its dining guide. A great up-to-the-minute resource for events and specials can be found at the Web site for Enews; it is updated every Wednesday. For everything you need to know about Salt Cay, there's a comprehensive Web site.

All About the Turks & Caicos **WhereWhenHow** (⊕www.Where WhenHow.com). **WhereWhenHow Dining Guide** (⊕www.WhereWhen How.tc). **Enews** (⊕www.TCIEnews. com). **Salt Cay** (⊕www.SaltCay.org).

INDEX

NOTES

NOTES

NOTES

NOTES

NOTES

NOTES

NOTES

NOTES

NOTES

NOTES

NOTES

NOTES

NOTES

ABOUT OUR WRITER

On a quest for the perfect beach, Ramona Settle decided on Turks and Caicos for her future retirement home. When she's not visiting the home with her family, she is making ice cream at her family's ice-cream stand in Virginia or taking pictures. Her photographs have been featured in the local *Times of the Islands* and *WhereWhenHow* magazines. She answers questions for travelers in the Fodors.com travel forums. Obsessed with travel, she visits the Turks & Caicos as often as she can and has Easter Island and South Africa on her wish list.